Right Recovery for You

Empowering You to Move Beyond Any Addictive or Compulsive Behavior

Right Recovery for You

Empowering You to Move Beyond Any Addictive or Compulsive Behavior

by Marilyn Maxwell Bradford
MSSW, MEd, CFMW

ACCESS
CONSCIOUSNESS®
PUBLISHING

Contents

Introduction

Hello, my name is Marilyn Bradford and I would like to invite you to a different possibility for moving beyond addiction.

My relationship with addiction began in early childhood. When I was seven years old, I was so addicted to sugar that my parents had to limit how much money I could spend per day on candy. Later I developed addictions to cigarettes, food and alcohol as well as certain behaviors like judging myself as wrong and trying to get it "right." What I didn't understand at the time was that I was choosing my addictions as a way to cope with not fitting in, feeling inherently wrong and being overwhelmed by the barrage of thoughts, feelings and emotions in my head. My recovery was a long and difficult process. Too bad I didn't know then what I know now!

I continued to drink, smoke and over- and-under-eat for the next few decades. Finally at a point when my marriage was failing and I was drinking myself into oblivion almost every night, I entered psychotherapy. I was fortunate to find a talented, non-traditional therapist who helped me begin to unravel my crazy web of lies and belief systems. After we worked together for a while, he sent me to a twelve-step program to help me stop drinking alcohol, as that seemed the best available option at the time. By then, my marriage had fallen apart, I was dealing with depression, and I was alienated from my family. However, I was beginning to have a glimpse of a life that was fuller and more exciting than anything I had thought possible.

Shortly thereafter, I entered a graduate program to become a therapist with a specialty in addiction. This program emphasized the importance of empowering people to have greater choice and control in their lives. Upon graduating, I worked for three-and-a-half years in a psychiatric hospital, where I ran the Adult Trauma Unit and worked with addicts. I then went into private practice. Over the next few years, I grappled with the paradox of working to stay sober by admitting my powerlessness and turning my life and will over to someone or something greater than me, while at the same time working from a theory grounded in the importance of empowering others.

I made a point of learning about other recovery programs, and I tried them all. Somehow applying someone else's answer to my addiction seemed to require an enormous amount of effort for an unsatisfactory result. Yes, I remained sober, but at a great cost to my being. I was told I had to have a permanent identity as an alcoholic and to put in hours of work each day to stay sober. The difficulty for me was that I desired to have a life that was based on far more than a restrictive recovery program—and I wished to offer that greater possibility to my clients.

What a relief it was to find Access Consciousness®! Finally there were truly empowering tools, techniques and processes I could apply to whatever was going on in my life, including my remaining issues with addiction. These tools were so effective that I began teaching them to my clients with amazing results. There was no longer a need to approach addiction using someone else's way. The tools enabled each of my clients to discover what true recovery was for him or her personally. The results were so dramatically different from those of psychotherapy or traditional addiction treatment that I asked Gary Douglas, the founder of Access Consciousness®, if we could start a program for addiction based on Access Consciousness®. This was the beginning of Right Recovery For You, LLC.

If you are willing to consider a radically different approach to addiction, this book is for you. Right Recovery for You does not offer a system that you fit yourself into. It does not tell you what to do or give you answers about your life. What it offers are tools, techniques, information and processes you can use to clear your issues with addiction and create a life beyond any addictive or compulsive behavior. This is your choice. It may seem a little scary at first, yet with courage and determination, you can move beyond the addictive behavior you thought would own you for the rest of your life.

Gratitude

Gary Douglas

The Right Recovery for You program would not have been possible without Gary Douglas, the founder of Access Consciousness®. Not only did he provide many of the tools, techniques and clearings; he has been aggressively supportive of my endeavors and all things related to Right Recovery for You. His brilliance, unflagging encouragement, true kindness and generosity of spirit have encouraged me to change, create and step up in ways I never dreamed were possible. I don't have words to adequately thank him, so I will just say: Immense gratitude to you, Gary Douglas. You rock!

Dr. Dain Heer

Dain has been an advocate of my work with Right Recovery For You from the beginning. Not only has he encouraged me to give classes, he has played a crucial part in my willingness to step into having and being more of me. He seemed to see, from the first time I met him, possibilities for me that went way beyond anything I could imagine. And he makes me laugh! Thank you so much Dain for your support and for your incredibly witty, off-the-wall sense of humor. You shine the light on what's stupid and insane in a way that allows it to change with ease.

Dona Haber

Many thanks to Dona, my amazing editor, for her inspired ideas and editing capacities, for unending cups of ginger tea, and for the ease with which she has walked me through the process of writing this book. And for the number of laughs and good times we've had with what some people might consider a heavy topic. Dona is a gem!

Simone Milasas

I would like to thank Simone for proactively supporting Right Recovery for You and going out of her way to encourage me in any way she could. I have so much respect for Simone—for her clarity, her wisdom and her capacity to see what is and where things can go. Her awareness of possibilities combined with her pragmatism and "let's do it now" approach to life has been a huge gift.

Suzy Godsey and Charlie

I would like to thank Suzy and and her dog Charlie for befriending me and giving me a wonderful place to stay while I was working on the book in Santa Barbara, and for all their kindness. In Access, we all know that Suzy is the nicest person in the world, and I came to realize that Charlie is the nicest dog in the world. Thank you both for creating such a lovely a space to rest, rejuvenate and have fun.

Blossom Benedict

Blossom has always been willing to ask me questions about Right Recovery and to share with me what she has done with her Right Voice for You program. She has a wonderful generosity of spirit and willingness to contribute. I also appreciate her joyfulness of being and the ease that she brings to whatever she is doing. Blossom always inspires a sense of "I'll have what she's having" and I've used that to motivate myself to choose more. Thank you Blossom!

Pam Houghteling,
Donnielle Carter, Cynthia Torp and Stephen Outram

I would also like to thank Pam, Donnielle, Cynthia and Stephen for being the incredibly professional, astute, creative and generous beings they are. Each of you has assisted me and Right Recovery For You in wonderful and helpful ways. Thank you so much!

Joy Voeth

Joy Voeth, head of Access Publishing, came to the project after it had started. Without her, it might never have been finished! Thank you, Joy, for your infinite patience, your creative suggestions, your unflagging support and your brilliance!

CHAPTER ONE

Myths and Lies About Addiction

As long as you're operating out of what you've been told addiction is—
and all the myths and lies that go along with that—
you will never be able to choose beyond it.

There is so much misinformation surrounding addiction that it is, at best, a highly confusing topic. Weighed down by lies and misinformation, many people who sincerely wish to walk away from their addictive or compulsive behavior suffer unnecessary failure and disappointment simply because they lack accurate information and effective tools. I'd like to start out by clearing up many of the most destructive myths and lies about addiction.

Let me ask you a question. Haven't you always known somewhere that many of the things you've been told about addiction were not true? Haven't you always known there must be tools that could actually work—and that there was a way to approach your addictive or compulsive behavior that would change everything and allow you to end it permanently?

You're right. Your knowing is correct. That's why I'm writing this book.

Paradigms

We all operate from paradigms in our lives. A paradigm is a set of assumptions, concepts, values and practices that constitute one's view of reality. It shapes the way a person sees the world. For example, all religions are paradigms. The standard model of physics is a paradigm. Western medicine is a paradigm. And there's a traditional paradigm for addiction treatment in our society.

Most of us believe that we operate from a place of being open-minded, and that is often true, at least to some extent. We are open-minded, we want to know the truth, and we're willing to look at the facts and consider other points of view. But sometimes there are places we simply will not go. There are ideas or possibilities we won't consider because we've bought into a paradigm that doesn't allow for the existence of that concept.

In the ancient world, people believed the Earth was shaped like a plane or a disk. Everyone bought into the paradigm that the world was flat. They thought, "Well, of course I'm open to new ideas, but I would never try to sail around the world because the world is flat, and everyone knows we would fall off the edge." The paradigm directed what the person could or could not believe—and what they could or could not choose.

Here's something important about paradigms—and this applies directly to conventional beliefs about addiction treatment and recovery. If the paradigm you believe in is not based on information that's true and workable, you can't possibly succeed with it. I see this happen over and over again with bright, amazing, wonderful people who have addictions. They consider themselves failures because the paradigm they used to try to stop their addictive or compulsive behavior was based on beliefs or assumptions that were not accurate. They accepted myths, ideas and systems that were flawed, invalid and untrue—and those myths and lies prevented them from having a satisfactory or successful result no matter how hard they tried.

Knowing What You Know

Before we move on, I want to acknowledge you for knowing what you know—because this knowing is a huge component in unlocking yourself from addiction. This book is not about giving you the answers. It's not going to tell you that you have to do it this way or you have to do it that way. The purpose of this book is to empower you by giving you effective tools and accurate information that you can use to make different life choices and change whatever behaviors you desire to change.

Whenever I present any information, I would like you to check in with yourself to see if it resonates for you. You know what's going to work for you—and what's not. You know what's true for you. You may respond to those statements by saying, "Help! I can't know what I know. I've tried doing that. I'm always wrong."

I understand that it may feel like that's the way it is, but it's not quite accurate. What's in the way of your knowing are all of the myths, lies and misinformation you have bought about addiction, who you are, what you're capable of and what your relationship to addiction is—and isn't.

So, let's begin by looking at some of the myths and lies about addiction that exist today.

But before we do that, I'd like you to take a moment and write down four to six things that you've been told about addiction. This can help clarify some of the paradigms you've bought into without even being aware of it.

Lie: Once an Addict, Always an Addict

The first lie is: Once an addict, always an addict. Once you have an eating disorder, you will always have a problem with food. Once you have a problem with alcohol, once you have a problem with abusive relationships, once you have a compulsion to rescue other people or whatever it is for you, you will always have a problem with that thing.

So, that's the first lie. You can move beyond any addictive or compulsive behavior that is currently limiting your life. You can have the life you've always known, dreamed and hoped you could have. Is it going to take work? Yes, it will. And if your target is to move beyond your addictive or compulsive behavior, sometimes you may be uncomfortable.

One of the mistakes many people make is judging that discomfort as bad or wrong. They've been led to believe that their target should be comfort. That's fine—if you want to maintain the life you've always had. But if you want something more, you should know that being uncomfortable is often a sign that things need to change or that you're breaking out of old patterns and paradigms. Discomfort is an indication of new possibilities and it can be your friend, not something you try to avoid.

Another falsehood related to the view, "Once an addict, always an addict" is the idea that you should identify with your compulsive or addictive behavior. Have you ever heard people say things like, "Hi, my name is Sally, and I'm an addict," "I'm Bob, I'm a smoker," or "My name is Susan, and I'm an alcoholic"? Taking on your addictive behavior as an identity ensures you will never get past it. Why is that? When you adopt the identity of being an addict, you have to engage in your addictive or compulsive behavior—because that's who you are. For example, if you identify yourself as an alcoholic, you have to drink—because that's what you do. You're someone who drinks alcohol.

Please stop identifying yourself with your addiction. Never say, "I'm a *this*." What you might say instead, as long as the addictive or compulsive behavior is a big part of your life, is, "I am currently choosing to engage in this behavior." That's all your addiction is. It's a behavior. And you're choosing to engage in it. I understand that at this point, it may feel like you don't have a choice. Please know you can change that too.

I also used to identify myself as an addict. Later I became aware that drinking was simply a behavior I had been choosing to escape from some things I did not want to be aware of. I remember going into a meeting one time, and instead of saying, "Hi, my name is Marilyn, and I'm an alcoholic," I said, "My name is Marilyn, and I've been addicted to anti-consciousness and unconsciousness, and I'm making different choices now." That gave me a great deal of freedom.

Here's a tool that will start you on the path to seeing your addictive or compulsive behavior as something you are choosing to engage in rather than something you are. It's a great first step because it creates distance between *who you are* and *what you are doing*.

Tool: Right Now I'm Choosing to Engage in This Behavior

Any time you find yourself engaging in the behavior that you know is limiting you, don't say to yourself, "Oh, here I go again. I'm a ____" and then fill in the blank with the word you use to describe yourself as an addict, whether it's *smoker, drinker, drug user, gambler* or anything else.

Instead say, "Okay, right now I'm choosing to engage in smoking or drinking (or whatever it is for you). I don't yet have all the tools and information I need to make different choices, but I know I'm going to change that at some point if that's what I desire to do." And you will be able to do that.

Lie: Addiction Only Happens to a Small, Dirty, Underground Population

Another one of the big myths and lies about addiction is not often spoken directly. It's the idea, more or less quietly put out there, that addiction only happens to a small, dirty, underground popula-

Use, Abuse and Addiction

You can take any substance or behavior, say alcohol, and you can use it, which would be, "Oh, it would be nice to have a glass of wine with dinner." You're choosing it because you're aware it would be pleasurable. There's no necessity to have it.

Or you can *abuse* a particular substance or behavior, which is where you're aware that you're choosing that particular thing to cope with a situation you don't feel like dealing with. It's not compulsive. It's, "Whew, I had such a rough day! My kid's teacher called because he got in trouble at school again. I know I need to sit down and talk with him, but you know what? I'm going to grab a couple of bowls of ice cream to calm me down because I can't deal with this right now and I need something to distract me." One of the keys to this kind of abuse is that you're using the substance or a behavior (in this case, the ice cream) in a way it's not meant to be used.

Then there is a form of *abuse* that is a transition between abuse and addiction. Say you have difficulty with your mother-in-law, and you have to go see her. You say to yourself, "I really don't want to go see my mother-in-law. I wonder what else I could do. I think I'll smoke a joint before I go over there." You do that, and then you think, "Wow, that helped a lot." The next time you have to see your mother-in-law or do something else you don't want to deal with, you remember that smoking a joint helped, so you do that, and after a while you automatically go to, "I think I'll smoke a joint first."

This is an example of how we can create the compulsivity of an *addiction*. We start out by using a substance or behavior—what we might call abusing it—as a way of helping us take care of something we don't want to deal with—and we decide that's the answer to dealing with such things. And then we allow it to take over and be the only way we can get relief on that particular topic. Rather than trusting ourselves to be present with a situation and do whatever is appropriate, we imbue a substance or behavior with the capacity to do for us what we've decided we can't do for ourselves.

tion. You know, the person who lives under the bridge or the drug addict who has flipped out. It's not anybody you know—and it's certainly not you or me. It's those few derelict people over there.

One of the things this lie does is to make addiction so taboo, secretive and shameful that nobody ever wants to look at it. It also creates a separation between you and those people. It's an "us vs. them" universe. You have to choose to belong to one group or the other, and that cuts off your awareness of what's going on with you and what might be possible. If you ever start to have the idea that you might have a problem with addiction, you quickly shut down that thought. For example, you may say to yourself, "I feel compulsive about this behavior. I don't know what to do." But you don't want to consider for a moment that you might be one of those awful, dirty, addicted people, so you immediately put that thought out of your mind. And that prevents you from making any changes.

Lie: Addiction Only Relates to a Few Substances or Behaviors

Most people believe addictions are limited to things like alcohol, drugs, cigarettes, food, gambling and sex. These are the obvious addictions. What if I told you that addiction can take many forms you never knew it could take? Some of those would be things like judging, being critical, needing to be right, making yourself wrong, figuring things out, feeling less-than, making other people's points of view more important than yours and having to have an answer to everything. Addiction can show up in relationships. It can show up with food and eating disorders, with exercise, with patterns of spending money or Internet use. What makes a particular substance or activity an addiction is not the *target* of it—the alcohol, the tobacco, the drug or the behavior—but the *way we use it*.

Addictions are engaged in by large numbers of people across all segments of the population. Some addictions are considered bad, terrible and wrong by the society at large, and some are considered positive or even admirable. If you have an addiction to work, an addiction to perfectionism, an addiction to being right, an addiction to looking good or an addiction to making lots of money, you might get a lot of support for that from this culture. That support might feel really good. But let me encourage you to ask two questions here:

- Is this behavior—this perfectionism or this workaholism or whatever it is—actually serving me well?

- Is this behavior helping me create the kind of life I would truly like to have?

You may have an addictive or compulsive behavior that looks good in society or one that doesn't. You may have one of the more subtle forms of addiction. You see people with these addictions every day. Have you ever known people who are addicted to trauma and drama? They cannot live their life without creating a trauma-drama of their own or participating in somebody else's. What makes that an addiction? It's absolutely compulsive. It's what they habitually revert to. It becomes a default setting in their life. Maybe you have an uncle or a cousin or a friend who *has* to judge you. They are addicted to judgment. If they're not judging, they don't know what to do with themselves. People can have an addiction to struggle. They can even have an addiction to being ill or to being a victim.

Now, why would a culture encourage or support any kind of addictive and compulsive behavior? Because it makes you controllable and predictable. All addictive behaviors eliminate your power of choice. Knowingly or unknowingly, you give up being the creator of your life and become the effect of a limited menu of choices.

Lie: The Best You Can Hope for Is to Manage the Symptoms of Addiction

Another lie is that the best you can hope for is to manage the symptoms of your addiction. That's what traditional treatment programs do. They tell you that you're going to have to work really hard for the rest of your life to manage the symptoms of your addiction—because you are an addict and you always will be. What if this lie gets perpetuated because people don't have the information they need to help you get to the core of what actually creates addiction?

The Right Recovery for You approach is about helping you get to the root cause of what created your addictive or compulsive behavior to begin with, so you can clear it permanently—not just manage the symptoms. Please don't buy the idea that the best you can hope for is to manage the symptoms.

Managing the symptoms of your addiction is like having a flat tire on your car and being given a fix-a-flat system that lasts for three hours. You're on a long journey and every three hours you have to get out and fix the flat. You're always obsessing about that. "Two hours and fifty minutes have gone by. I have to get out and fix the flat." You are faced with a lifetime of fixing the flat when you buy the lie that the best you can do is manage the symptoms. You can do far more than that!

One of the untruths born out of the belief that the best you can do is manage the symptoms is the idea that recovery means stopping the addictive or compulsive behavior completely. The Right Recovery for You approach doesn't impose a pre-determined target on people. I work with clients to create a target that's right for them—a target that *they* choose. That is our measure of success. For many people, "success" may mean not ever engaging in what had been an addictive or compulsive behavior, but for others, it may mean being able to have a few drinks or to smoke a cigarette from time to time.

Results of Traditional Treatment Programs

The traditional approach to handling addiction is often promoted by doctors, therapists, counselors and the judicial system. Have you ever wondered how effective this approach actually is?

I've found that for many people, it's often not very successful. If you're interested in looking at the success rates of traditional treatment programs, I encourage you to research them on the Internet. Google is a good tool. What I discovered is that the success rate ranges from five percent to twelve or thirteen percent. And what's rarely considered or researched is the number of people who choose to quit in a non-traditional way.

If you were ill, would you unquestioningly accept treatment from a doctor or a program that had a success rate of between five and thirteen percent?

Lie: You're Weak, Selfish, Dishonest, Immoral, Sinful, Wicked, Criminal and Unethical for Having This Addiction

In other words, if you have an addiction other than a socially accepted one, you're very, very wrong. The most popular addiction treatment model asks you to judge yourself on a daily basis to see if your behavior has been selfish, self-seeking, dishonest or based in fear. You're asked to continuously look at where you're wrong.

I've found that many people with addictive and compulsive behaviors are far from being selfish. They're some of the most kind and caring people I've ever met. Many of them would rather take on the poison in life than have it show up for someone else. This may be true for you, as well. If it is, please acknowledge this truth about yourself. Do not buy the lie that you are wrong, bad and weak and that you have perpetrated terrible things on the people around you. Everyone around the "addict" plays a part in any addiction drama, and they too have choice.

Years ago, I worked as a psychotherapist at a psychiatric hospital. One of the concepts that we employed in treating people was the principle of the "identified patient." People would come into the hospital and we would be told that they had depression or alcoholism or this or that condition. The person's family would be there and they'd say, "Oh yes, Johnny has this problem. He has been a worry and a pain for all of us. He has caused so many problems. Uh-huh."

We'd always think, "Hmm, okay, Johnny is the identified patient. I wonder what's *really* going on here? I wonder who really has the problem?" And, as we worked with the family, we would often find that while everyone was making Johnny wrong and pointing their fingers at him, Johnny wasn't actually the problem. When we delved into the family dynamic more deeply, we discovered that Johnny's addictive behavior kept the family system going. If Johnny quit being the wrong one, the bad one, then guess what? Everybody else would have to look at *his* or *her* own behavior, and in most of the families we worked with, nobody wanted to do that. That's why they created their Johnny as the identified patient.

I once worked with a young woman whose family agreed she had a problem with alcohol, and they saw her as weak, selfish and immoral for having her addiction. After she and I worked together for a while, she disclosed that she had been sexually abused over a long period of time by an uncle who was very close to the family. I realized that the family was, to one degree or another, aware of this abuse, but nobody wanted to bring it up. No one wanted to address the fact that the uncle had been—and was still—making advances toward this young woman. So, instead of dealing with that, they set it up that she was the one with the problem because of her drinking. Once my client began to realize the truth of that, we were able to begin to change things, and she was eventually able to stop drinking, which was her target.

Many people discover that their addiction permitted them to survive abusive situations until they could get some help. I recently worked with a woman who had come from a very abusive past. She was harshly judging herself for eating large amounts of food every night. When I asked her what contribution the eating had been to her, her response was immediate. She said the eating was a terrible, bad, horrible, awful thing and it had caused her to be fat and unattractive.

I asked her, "If you hadn't had all of that food, if you hadn't done that "over"eating, what would your life be like today? She burst into tears and said, "If I hadn't had the food to help me deal with the abuse, I probably would have committed suicide by now." Once she was able to see that her "over"eating was the best way she had at the time for coping with the abuse, she began to make changes that led her to different relationship with food and her body.

I worked with another person who said that his use of drugs had helped him to not kill himself or someone else until he was able to get into an environment where help was possible. So, please do not judge your addictive behavior. Instead, you might ask yourself these questions, "Was my addictive behavior the best coping mechanism I had until now? And am I now ready to make some real changes?"

One of the most unfortunate and destructive things about the lie that you are wrong, bad and weak is that it plays into a primary addiction you developed a very, very long time ago. What I'm saying here is that the current target of your addiction was preceded by a primary addiction: the addiction to judging yourself, being wrong and feeling overwhelmed by what you saw as the insanities of this reality. You're bound to the current target of your addiction by the pain of believing that you are wrong and you must judge yourself.

The primary addiction to judging yourself and being wrong is discussed at greater length in chapter three. I want to mention it here, though, because the lie that you're weak, selfish, dishonest—or whatever the judgment is—contributes to the ongoing difficulty of ending any addictive or compulsive behavior.

Lie: Everyone in Your Life Actually Wants You to End Your Addictive or Compulsive Behavior

One of the biggest lies out there is that everyone in your life actually desires for you to end your addictive or compulsive behavior. The truth is, many don't. They don't because they're used to you being in a one-down position. They're accustomed to you being the less-than person, and even if you're hiding your addictive behavior, they pick up that you're judging yourself as wrong. Some are actually happy for you to have an addiction, even if it's largely unconscious. That sounds cruel and I don't mean it to be so; it's simply something I've seen over and over again. If you are identified as the one who has the problem, then the people close to you don't have to examine their behavior.

There's another concept that was used in the psychiatric hospital where I used to work. It was called change-back, and I often see it when I work with people who have addictions. As the person begins to move away from his or her addictive or compulsive behavior and makes the choice to show up as who he or she truly is, the family or significant other begins to react in strange ways. They may have been saying for a decade, "We just want Mary to get better." Then, as soon as Mary starts to move away from her addictive behavior and can no longer be classified as the wrong one or the bad one that everyone needs to disparage, help or spend time and energy on, the family finds subtle or not-so-subtle ways of encouraging Mary to go back to her addictive or compulsive behavior. Why? Because they don't really want her to change.

I experienced this myself. My first husband often expressed concern that I was drinking too much. He frequently told me I needed to get help and talked about the ways my behavior was adversely affecting our marriage. After a while, I began to believe him and I started making efforts to drink less. I noticed two things: One, I was moderately successful, although not as successful as I had hoped, in drinking less; and two, the less I drank the more he would say things like, "I can see you're really stressed. (I worked at his office.) Why don't you go home now and open a bottle of champagne?" This was very confusing! It took me a while to see that he actually needed me to be dependent on alcohol. He was aware, on some level, that once I stepped into being more of me, once I had a glimpse of what I might be capable of, I would no longer be satisfied with our little life and my "less-than" position. He was correct!

If you have one or two people in your life who truly desire to empower you—and that's what this should be about—count yourself lucky and receive from them. And know that there may also be people who appear to care about you and who say that they would like you to end your addictive or compulsive behavior yet would prefer that you didn't upset the apple cart.

I bring up this lie, not as a downer, but as something to be aware of. Once you begin to step into being more of you, you may make the people close to you uncomfortable. Everything is interconnected, so when one part of the system changes—and that's you—the other part has to change and adjust—that's them. They may not desire to do that, and they may say to you in words or energetically, "Wait a minute. You just stepped out of your box. When you're in that box, I know who you are. I can control you. You're predictable. I don't have to worry that you might show up as somebody else."

Are you truly willing to stay in your box? Or would you like something greater for your life? My guess is you wouldn't be reading this book if you didn't actually wish to have something greater.

Lie: You Are Powerless Over Your Addiction

This lie has come out of many people's experience with trying not to engage in their addictive behavior of choice—not to take a drink, smoke a cigarette or pair up with yet another abusive man or woman. On the surface, it may seem to make sense, but let's consider it from a different point a view.

If I'm standing directly in front of a brick wall, and I really want to get through it, but I have no tools, I'm going to feel powerless. I'll be thinking, "I can't get through this brick wall! Help! There's no way through!"

Now, suppose someone comes along and offers me some information. They say, "Hey, Marilyn, what if you step back from the wall? What do you see?"

Stepping back, I can see that the wall is only five feet long and I can go around it, or I see that while it's seven feet tall, someone has given me a ladder and I can go over it. I'm not actually powerless at all; I just didn't have a true perspective on the situation or the tools to deal with it.

This is also the case with any addictive or compulsive behavior. It may seem that you are powerless in the moment, but as you change your perspective and start using the tools and information in this book, you will find that the addictive behavior is not what you thought it was, nor is it as formidable as you have been led to believe.

The great difficulty with buying the lie that you are powerless over your addiction is that it puts you in the position of being the *effect* in your life rather than the creator of your life. It strips you of your power. This lie puts you in the position of needing an expert, a dogma, an answer or a program that is imposed on you in order for you to have any way of dealing with your addictive or compulsive behavior.

You might ask yourself these questions:

- If I have bought the lie that I am powerless over my addictive or compulsive behavior, where else have I bought the lie of powerlessness?

- Am I actually powerless or am I just lacking good, workable information and tools?

Have you often found yourself looking for the next "right" program, book or expert who will have *the* answer to all of the things about yourself and your life that you have decided you are powerless over and can't change? What if you could choose from an array of tools and information that allowed you to change any part of your life you wished to change? What if you could customize the material for you rather than buying, hook, line and sinker, somebody else's dogma? Please be very careful any time you decide you are powerless over anything. If you find yourself doing that, ask yourself the questions above.

The idea that you are powerless over your addiction leads into the next lie.

Lie: Only Someone or Something Outside of You Can End Your Addiction

Why do we tend to look outside of ourselves for answers? Well, isn't that what we've been taught to do our whole life? We have to do what Mom and Dad say because they "know better." We have to believe everything our teachers, religious leaders, doctors, politicians and elders tell us because they are the experts and we can't possibly know more than they do. That's the beginning of the lie of depending on someone or something outside of you to end your addiction. The truth is it's not that you don't have the power; it's that no one has ever assisted you in developing it.

Here's the thing: If you buy a lie and try to make it true, you are not only doomed to failure, you also create anxiety in your life because part of you knows, somewhere, that it's a lie. It's like losing your key and knowing on some level that it's inside the house, but the experts are telling you that people only lose their keys outside of their houses. So what do you do? You spend all your time looking for it in your lawn—even though you know you misplaced it somewhere inside your house.

Haven't you always known, even if you didn't feel that you could trust your knowing, that you were the one with the answers you needed? You know more about you than anyone else in the world. What if you began to trust your knowing now?

You may be saying, "I can't trust my knowing. I've been wrong my whole life." Actually, there was a time when you allowed yourself to know what you knew. When you were an infant, you knew what you needed. You cried when you needed food, when you wanted to be held or when you needed your diaper changed. The difficulty is that as you grew up, you were not acknowledged. Your needs were diminished or you were made to feel that your knowing was wrong, and you decided you couldn't know what you knew. You can regain this capacity. It may take some practice, but as you begin to trust yourself to know what you know, you will find yourself being more comfortable in that awareness.

Lie: Addiction Is a Disease

Let's look at another lie about addiction, the lie that addiction is a disease. It's a disease? Is addiction a disease like cancer or malaria?

Has the statement that addiction is a disease always sounded wacky to you? When I first heard it, I wondered why anyone would draw that conclusion. Then I realized that much of the medical and treatment culture is invested in addiction being a disease. As a matter

25

of fact, most addiction treatment is financed by states, local governments and public and private health insurers to the tune of billions of dollars per year. If addiction were not considered a disease, these groups would not pay for individual drug treatment programs, outpatient recovery programs or hospital stays. Addiction has to be a disease for everyone in the business to make tons of money. I'm not trying to make these people wrong. They may be very good-hearted, caring individuals who need to make a living. So, consciously or unconsciously, they go along with the idea that addiction is a disease.

But addiction is *not* a disease. You are *not* sick. Addiction is an entrenched pattern of avoidance and/or escape from a life that appears to be too overwhelming, confusing and painful. It is a place people go to not exist, to not experience the pain of self-judgment and to avoid the sense of being inherently wrong.

If you see addiction in this way, you'll understand that you have the freedom to change it. You will be able to get a sense of how you created your addiction in the first place and how you ended up in this bewildering, apparently no-choice situation.

One of the things that rankles me about seeing addiction called a disease is that it puts everyone with an addiction into a victim position—because according to our culture, if you have a disease, there's little to nothing you can do about it. It's something that just happens to you. You then have to go see an expert—the doctor—who will "cure" you. Basically the disease model is saying, "You don't know what you're doing. You have to come to us, the experts, and we'll give you the answer."

The only expert about all of this is you. You are the expert on you. Does that mean you don't listen to anyone else? No. You may lack information. For instance, when I have difficulty with a computer, I go to a computer expert. Why? Not because I need someone to run my life, but because a computer expert has information and can show me tools that will help me operate my computer. I look for someone who is not trying to lord it over me or show me how I'm wrong. I look for someone who will say, "Hey, I have a whole bunch of information and tools in this area. Let me show you what I've got so you can use what's going to work for you."

That's why I've written *Right Recovery for You*. I would love to see you empowered so you can change anything in your life that you would like to change—and that includes any addictive or compulsive behavior that's stopping you, limiting you or preventing you from being the true gift that you are.

What You Can Do
When You're Drawn to Engage in Your Addictive
or Compulsive Behavior

Pause, Ask Yourself Some Questions

When you find yourself experiencing a craving or desire to engage in your addictive or compulsive behavior, here are some questions you can ask yourself. It's helpful to write your answers down.

- What event occurred just prior to my desire to engage in my addictive or compulsive behavior?
- What was my reaction to that event?

  (Example: My husband/wife called me an idiot and I went to the wrongness of me.)

- What thoughts did I have?
- What feelings did I have?
- What was I aware of that I didn't want to be aware of?

  (Example: That I was back in my old pattern. I was making my husband's/wife's opinion of me greater than what I know to be true of myself.)

- What action could I have taken that might have interrupted this pattern?

When you pause and write your answers down, you're interrupting the behavior, which is what these initial tools are about.

Put the Behavior Off

Another thing that you can do to interrupt the behavior is to put it off, even if it's just for twenty minutes. Say to yourself, "I'm going to give myself permission to engage in my addictive or compulsive behavior, but first I'm going to take a twenty-minute break. If I still desire to do it after twenty minutes, I'll do it."

If you do choose to engage in the behavior after twenty minutes, give yourself the gift of not judging yourself.

When you put the behavior off for twenty minutes or more, you'll see you actually have some choice. You can choose whether to engage in it—or not. Initially you may not feel that you have complete choice, but I would like you to get that you do have some choice—or you wouldn't be able to put it off at all.

Ask Some More Questions

Sit down and say to yourself: "Okay, I may engage in my behavior in twenty minutes. Before I do that, I'm going to ask myself some questions and write down the answers."

- What have I decided will happen if I don't engage in the behavior at this time?
- Have I made the consequences of not engaging in the behavior bigger or more powerful than me?
- On a scale of 1-10, how stressful is the idea of not engaging in the behavior?
- Could I actually tolerate the consequences of not engaging in the behavior with more ease than I thought?

- What awareness am I trying to avoid here, by engaging in the addictive or compulsive behavior?

- What would it be like if I were willing to have that awareness?

- If I had no history with this behavior, how would I relate to it?

- How much of what I am doing with my addictive or compulsive behavior is about the past and everything I've decided the past is—or isn't?

The past doesn't have to dictate what your life is today. You can choose something different.

If You Do Choose to Engage in Your Addictive or Compulsive Behavior, Do It with Awareness

Allow yourself to become aware with each puff of a cigarette, each bite of cake or each sip of alcohol. Ask yourself, "Okay, I've had this. Do I actually desire more?" Becoming aware of the behavior you're choosing to engage in creates a space where the behavior becomes less compulsive for you.

These questions and exercises are simply suggestions. Choose the ones that work for you. They will help you to become more conscious and aware of what's going on with your addictive behavior.

Please remember to write down your answers to the questions. You're going to get a lot of amazing information each time you do this. And you're going to begin to see that you have some choice and that you can (at least to some degree at this point in your recovery) separate from your addictive or compulsive behavior, which will allow you to see it from a different perspective.

CHAPTER TWO

The Antidote to Addiction

The more you have of you, the more you step into being who you truly are, the less addictive and compulsive behaviors can exist.

An addiction is like a poison to your being in the sense that every time you engage in it, it diminishes or negates your capacity to be present, spontaneous, joyful, and productive; in other words, it diminishes or negates your capacity to be who you truly are.

Many people have bought the idea that the antidote to addiction is about looking outside of themselves for some sort of remedy, answer or one-size-fits-all program. Or they may believe it's about fighting the addiction, judging themselves as wrong for engaging in it or attempting to control their behavior. But that's not it. The antidote to addiction is more fundamental and potent than any of those things. It's about reclaiming all the parts of yourself that you have disowned, let go of or repressed. You, being you, is the actual antidote to addiction. This doesn't mean that you might not need some initial assistance in the process of recovering, discovering and creating yourself. What it does mean is that in the end, you can have and be all that is required to come to a place of choice with your addictive or compulsive behavior.

Let's take an example of this, using your body. Say you had some kind of an accident, and both your arms and legs were broken. And let's say, for some strange reason, you broke your own arms and legs on purpose—perhaps because it made you less powerful and you could fit in better. If you created that situation, you would need help for a while. But in the end, you wouldn't need the help anymore because you would have healed and restored the power of you to you. You'd say to the help, "Bye-bye, don't need you anymore, sayonara, see you later," and you would be the captain of your own ship again.

If, on the other hand, you decided you were so wrong and weak that you had to live with broken arms and legs the rest of your life, you would need outside help for forever. You would never restore yourself to the power and potency you truly are—because you'd be buying the lie that your broken legs and arms and all of the ways you had handicapped yourself were permanent. You would always require an outside sense of power. You might have even decided that this was the way it was supposed to be.

This example has huge implications for addiction, because the truth is you have handicapped yourself. If you have an addictive or compulsive behavior, you have handicapped yourself by denying many of your talents and abilities, by diminishing the power you have or by cutting off all of the parts of you that were deemed unacceptable by parents, family members, teachers and other authority figures in your life.

We are all born with different temperaments, talents and abilities, but if your family and the people around you didn't value those qualities, you may have felt that you needed to cut them off so you would be acceptable. Maybe you were curious and smart and you asked a lot of questions, but your family didn't value being smart. Your questions made people uncomfortable, so you shut down that part of yourself.

Maybe you were athletic or very active. You could do six or seven things at a time, and you loved it, but people told you had too much energy and you needed to quiet down and control yourself. Or perhaps you were artistic or unconventional, and that was not the way you were supposed to be in your family. You were expected to settle down and get a well-paying job or to carry on the family business, so you put your abilities or wonderful, wild ideas aside and forgot about them.

Or you may have been sensitive and aware, and you were told, "You're just too sensitive." You picked up things that no one wanted to talk about. You said, "Mom, Uncle Billy feels weird," and you were told, "He's our family. You're not allowed to say things like that." Or maybe someone was being mean to you, but if you said anything, the response was, "You're a crybaby." You got the idea no one wanted to listen, so you stopped talking.

Many kids feel a need to diminish themselves because they're told they have a responsibility to think of everyone else first. I spoke with a friend who told me that when he was a boy, the first thing he did when he woke up in the morning was to try and figure out what his mom and dad needed, what his grandma needed and what his teacher needed. He put himself so far down on the list that he rarely got to what *he* needed. Was that true for you? Were you expected to put everybody else's needs in front of your own? That was another way of diminishing you, because no one acknowledged that you had the right to have your own needs and desires. And more than that, because you learned not to put your needs out there, you may not be in touch with what they actually are, to the point that it becomes easier to figure out what everybody else needs than to be aware of what you require.

The Process of Diminishing Yourself

If you have had experiences like these, you may have concluded that who you are is not acceptable, and you may have closed down your beautiful exuberance and joyfulness, your intelligence, talents, interests and inclinations. I call this the process of cutting off the parts and pieces of you. This process starts very early on in our lives.

Can you see how shutting off your innate abilities and interests and ignoring your needs makes you like the person with the broken arms and legs? Except in this case, you may not even know those parts of you are gone. You may have a vague memory of them, but you don't realize that you're only operating at ten to twenty percent of who you really are. The amazing thing is, I'll bet you probably function well with that ten to twenty percent. Imagine for a moment how well you would function if you were operating at even fifty percent of you. How about seventy-five percent? Would you be willing to have that? Would you be willing to have a hundred percent of you? The more you step into who you truly are, the more addiction becomes a moot point.

You are the antidote to addiction, because when you are willing to have all of you, you don't have to fight your addiction; it just fades away. There's no reason to have it. Or as one of my clients said, "You know, Marilyn, I haven't thought about doing drugs for weeks. I'm having so much fun with me back that I just forgot about it."

That's what I would like for you. I'd like for you to recover you and to feel so powerful in your being that you just forget about your addictive or compulsive behavior. I'd like you to know that just by being you, your addiction can become irrelevant. There won't be any reason to talk about it any longer—not when you are present, not when you are willing to be aware, not when you are living the life you desire as opposed to the life you've been told is the only appropriate one for you.

"That Just Doesn't Seem Possible"

At this point, you may be saying, "That just doesn't seem possible." Or you may be thinking, "Marilyn, you've been talking about paradigms, traditional treatment programs, me becoming more of me and knowing what I know. That's all fine, but what about my addiction? I feel kind of panicked, like I need to fight it head-on right now; otherwise, nothing will ever change for me."

I've heard this from many clients. I'd like to ask you to take a look at what happens when you strongly focus your attention on something and begin to fight it. Say your tooth hurts. You keep running your tongue over it, and every time you do that, you think, "Ouch, this really hurts." The more you focus on your tooth, the more it hurts. It works the same way with addictive or compulsive behavior. The more you focus on it with an energy that's charged, the more powerful it seems to become.

Have you ever noticed what happens when your child, a partner or a co-worker, picks a fight with you and you jump in and fight back? If you're like I used to be, you may think it's going to accomplish something positive, but in the end, it only strengthens the negative relationship between you and the other person and leaves the issues unresolved. The same is true with fighting your addiction. If you fight your addiction, all you accomplish is to judge yourself harshly and strengthen your tie to the addictive behavior, which in turn, leads to more pain about being wrong and an increased desire to escape into addiction.

Changing the Energy That You Are

I'm suggesting an approach that isn't about focusing on the addiction or fighting it. As you step in to becoming more of you, you change the energy that you are. Doing that—changing the energy that you are—allows you to move away from your addictive or compulsive behavior because addiction can only exist with an energy that is vibrationally compatible. Let me help bring clarity to this by asking you to do a little exercise.

Right now, imagine yourself engaging in your addictive or compulsive behavior. Really immerse yourself in what that feels like.

Can you get a sense of the energy of it? Hold that for a moment and then imagine a situation that is fairly neutral. It may be sitting around and watching TV, having your breakfast, or getting into your car. Get the energy of that.

Now remember a time when you were feeling joyful and happy to be alive. Get the energy of that. Really immerse yourself in that energy and stay there for a few moments. Have you lightened up at all? Is there a smile on your face? Can you feel your body relaxing? That's the energy that allows you to step out of your addictive behavior and create new possibilities. What I'd like you to get here is that you can make the choice to change the energy you are being, and through that choice, you can alter your relationship with your addictive or compulsive behavior. Choosing to change the energy is a huge component in ending addiction. Change your energy, and addiction can no longer exist.

Changing the Dense, Contracted Energy of Addiction

When people are looking to change an addictive or compulsive behavior, they sometimes think they need to have an intense experience in order to make the change. They're in search of something that matches the density and intensity of their addiction. For instance, I know people who have said things like, "I just went to a bodyworker and she did something so intense. I know that it's going to help me with my addiction."

What I see is that the bodyworker matched the intensity and density of the person's addictive behavior; she didn't facilitate the client in changing his or her energy. That bodywork is not going to do anything for the client because it didn't address the client's energy at all. In some ways, that sort of experience keeps the addictive behavior more entrenched. Here's an example of what I mean: If you have an addiction to trauma-drama, you're going to keep creating trauma-drama in your life. You might be one of those people who asks, "How come all of this bad stuff always happens to me?" Well, if you are the energy of trauma-drama, you are going to create more trauma-drama. You have to become a different energy, an energy of ease, in order to change the situation. If you do intense and perhaps painful bodywork to help you end your addiction to trauma-drama, you might think you're doing something that will help you stop creating it, but really, you're just locking more trauma-drama into your body.

Part of the antidote to addiction—to you being the antidote to addiction—is changing the dense, contracted energy of your addiction to an energy that is lighter and more expansive. That's what awareness is. It's being present with what is. It's being in the lightness and expansiveness of that expression.

I know that sounds counter-intuitive because we think, "I've got to be strong, intense and powerful to overcome my addiction. That's what it's going to take to win out over it." And that just isn't true at all. The more you have of you, the more light, expanded and aware you are, the less addictive and compulsive behaviors can exist. They can't exist because those behaviors are characterized by a density and a contraction that's dependent on you not being you. That dense energy cannot co-exist with the expansiveness you create when you are being who you truly are.

The more you step into being you, the more you rediscover and recover the many talents, abilities and facets of you that you've cut off or disowned. I've seen scores of people do it. Yes, it takes time. But you can begin to restore the power of you today. And that's what we're going to start working on.

Sometimes people say to me, "Well, what you're saying is fine, but I already did that work in therapy."

I've been a psychotherapist for many years, and I do very little of it any more because in my experience, therapy doesn't usually help people become who they truly are; instead, it tends to help them make a better adjustment to the requirements of their family, culture and community. Whether it's about a job, a relationship or some form of self-expression, therapy is generally designed to help you find your appropriate place in society. Mental health is often measured by a person's willingness to change and adapt to what has been decided are appropriate behaviors, responsibilities and roles. There is an unspoken agreement that the client should be helped to see how he or she can better fit into the accepted paradigms. If that requires you to divorce yourself from the parts of you that don't fit, it's considered an acceptable and necessary sacrifice on your part for the good of the whole. If you don't do that, you are considered self-ish. People often come away from therapy saying things like, "Well, that's just the way it is. That's reality. I have to adjust. That's just life on life's terms." Actually, you don't have to adjust! You can choose to do so if it adds to your life—but you don't have to. You have other choices.

Let's look at some of the other factors that influence and support the process of diminishing you.

Going to School

How was school for you? Was going to school another experience of not fitting in? We're not linear beings, but we're made to believe that we should live in a linear fashion—line up, fifty minutes of math, fifty minutes of English, fifty minutes of social studies. Now go outside on the playground and have fun for fifty minutes. Did that work for you? It didn't work for me and I bet it didn't work for you either.

Does your mind go from A to B to C? Or does it go from A to M and back to B? What if that's the way a highly creative mind works? Did you shut all of that off in an attempt to be linear because that's what was required? And how did you like sitting in those rows of desks and standing in line and being still while you waited for lunch? Was that fun for you or did it require you to shut yourself down in order to comply?

Another way schools deaden the natural curiosity and creativity of students is by expecting everyone to have the same (correct) answer. "What's wrong with that?" you might ask. "Isn't that why we go to school—to learn the answers?" If you look at what an answer does, you'll see that it, too, requires you to shut down the energy. It's the end of the exploration of what might be possible. Say you were expected to have an answer to the question, "What were the causes of the U.S. Civil War?" and you were given a list of five things to memorize. You'd say, "Oh, okay, I can memorize those five things and put them on the test." But if you believe the complexity of the answer is those five things, you never ask, "What else could it have been? What are we not looking at here?" You shut down your inquisitive mind in favor of a list of five answers from the teacher that may be inaccurate or incomplete.

That's what school, with its focus on answers, does to students. Unless you had a very different experience from most people, school deactivated the inquisitive, curious part of you, the questioning part of you. And the questioning part of you is a huge factor in what helps you to be the antidote to addiction. That's because questions allow you to look beyond what appears to be true as the only option. They allow you to see other possibilities.

Let's go on with this just a little bit more. Were you made wrong for multi-tasking in school? Many kids have way too much energy to sit still and do one boring thing at a time. Was that true for you? Were you labeled, criticized or even drugged because your natural inclination was to do many different things at once?

Many kids faced with the pressure to fit in choose to shut down their energy and adopt the role of the good little girl or boy—or else they choose to become the rebel. Neither role allows for the true self to show up because both roles are sets of predetermined reactions. So, whether you were being a good boy or girl or the rebel, it is still not about you being you. Being you is outside of any system or particular adopted role. Being you is not about resisting and reacting to something, nor is it aligning and agreeing with it. It's simply about what's true for you. And once again, that goes back to you knowing what you know.

And wasn't that another thing that was unacceptable in school? You weren't allowed to know what you knew? You were required to show your work. Say you were doing a multiple choice math test. The answers were: a) 3 ¼, b) 9 ¾, c) 7 ½, d) 5. You looked at them and said, "Oh! It's 9 ¾!"

Did the teacher ask you, "How did you get the answer to that math problem?"

You said, "I don't know. I just got it."

If you couldn't prove your knowing in a linear manner, your answer wasn't acceptable. The teacher said, "Well, if you can't prove your work, you must have been cheating or copying." Did you secretly know what you knew, but you also realized that you weren't allowed to simply "know things," so you tried to do it their way?

This kind of experience diminishes the inborn knowing we all have. Have you ever been driving on the freeway and you just knew to get off at a particular exit, even though your directions told you to get off two exits later? Then you found out that you had avoided a huge traffic jam due to road construction or a big wreck. If someone had asked you, "Why are you getting off here?" you wouldn't have been able to explain. You just knew to do it. That's what knowing is. It's not logical and it's not something that is acceptable or acknowledged by many people—especially in school.

Being Who You Are "Supposed" to Be

As you grew older, did you try to discern what society had decided was a successful adult? How much information was out there telling you what that meant? Did you get the message, "You know you're successful if you earn a lot of money, have 2.2 children, live in a house with a white picket fence and go to PTA meetings"? Was that fulfilling for you? Or did you have a sense there might be more in life for you than that?

All of this is by way of saying that in every phase of your life, there are people and institutions that would like you to suppress who you *actually* are so you fit into being who you are *supposed* to be. Buying into that creates the core of addiction. It's incredibly painful to not be who we truly are.

Many years ago, I had an indoor-outdoor cat. This was a courageous, wild kitty. She would go out to hunt and come into the house carrying a squirrel that was the same size she was. One day I couldn't find her anywhere. I looked and I looked. Finally I discovered her hunkered down behind the bathroom door. Something bad had happened to her, but it wasn't clear what it was. We took her to the vet. She had some minor injuries—maybe she'd been hit by a car or had a run-in with a dog. Whatever it was really scared her. It told her that being courageous was wrong, and she contracted herself down into a tiny being that was about one tenth of who she truly was. We had to work with her for a while to help her get herself back, and she did once again become the courageous, wild kitty she had always been.

That same thing happens to us. Something occurs in our life, and we think that contracting down is a good idea. A lot of us contracted in childhood because it was the "safe" thing to do. It made us feel less vulnerable. You didn't want to be around when Dad was in a bad mood. You thought, when the bully was on the school playground, that making yourself small was the best thing to do. And are you still doing that? Are you still making yourself unnoticeable in one way or another? Is that actually serving you well or is it just reinforcing the idea that you are powerless?

Exercise: Expanding Out

This exercise is designed to help you move from a contracted space to a much more expansive one. Most of us are accustomed to having our energy be very contracted, but that contraction actually creates huge limitations. When you step into being the space you can truly be, you have a far greater platform from which to create and generate your life. That space also allows you to deal more easily with all that comes to and at you from this reality.

Before starting this exercise, please be aware that the being is not inside the body. The body is inside the being!

Directions:

(You may wish to record this exercise so that you can listen to the instructions.)

- Find a comfortable place to sit where you won't be disturbed.

- Now take a deep breath in, and slowly release it.

- And take another deep breath in and slowly release it. Allow your body to relax, letting all of the tension go.

- Now I would like to you expand your being outside your body by eight to ten inches. You don't have to *try* to do it— just ask and you create it.

- Take a moment to be aware of what that's like for you.

- Now expand out to fill whatever room you are in. Take a moment to be aware of what that's like for you.

- Now expand out to fill the entire building you are in. Take a moment to see what that's like for you.

- Now expand out to be a big as the town you are in.
- Now expand out fifty miles in every direction, including down into the earth.
- Now expand out 200 miles in every direction, including down into the earth.
- Now expand out 1,000 miles in every direction, including down into the earth.
- Now expand out 5,000 miles in every direction, including down into the earth.
- Now expand out 20,000 miles in every direction, including down into the earth.
- Now expand out 100,000 miles in every direction including down into the earth.
- Now expand out 500,000 miles in every direction including down into the earth.
- Now expand out as far as you would like to go, including down into the earth. Take a moment to notice the energy and space you are being. Hang out here for a moment or two or more. What is this like for you?
- Now open your eyes, maintaining as much of the expansion as you would like. How is that for you? Are you willing to be this much space on a regular basis? You can, you know.

The willingness to be space will create much more ease for you. I encourage you to practice this exercise every day until it becomes easy for you to immediately be the space you desire to be. Initially, you may only be able to do a small portion of this exercise. Don't worry if you can't seem to do it right away. It may take some practice. When I first learned to do this exercise, I did it every morning and evening. You may wish to do that as well.

This is a great exercise to use when you notice that someone is judging you—or when you are judging yourself—because nothing contracts you like judgment does. The more space you're willing to be, the less judgments will stick to you. That's important—because judgments lead you to judge yourself as wrong, and the pain of being wrong and not fitting in is one of the big reasons you go into the place of addictive or compulsive behavior to begin with.

Two Common Judgments

In the following section, I'm going to talk about two common judgments that society applies to people with addictions. If you buy either of them as true, you will contract and diminish yourself again.

"You're Selfish"

People who have addictive or compulsive behaviors are often accused of being selfish. In fact, in some of the traditional treatment programs, it's one of the things people with addictions are routinely told: "You're selfish."

Selfish. That's a bad thing, right? Well, maybe not. Selfishness can be a very good thing. If an infant weren't selfish, if it never expressed its needs or desires regardless of what was going on with other people, it might never get fed or changed. When you deny yourself and continually put others before you, you're not in the equation of your own life. You're just there to be and do what other people need for you to be and do. You lose the awareness of your own needs and wants—and how can you be you when you are unaware of those things?

What most people mean when they accuse you of being selfish is that you're not being the person they want you to be, and you're not fulfilling their needs. You're selfish if you want to spend the day reading and don't wish to run errands with them. You're selfish if you don't live up to what they have decided your responsibilities and obligations are. They say that you are wrong and you are hurting them. They say, "You're putting yourself first. You need to put yourself aside for me." Actually, you need to put yourself first! If you don't put yourself first, you cannot be the true gift you are to the world. That's a far cry from being selfish.

I once had a client who had been labeled a drug addict. His wife considered herself the long-suffering victim. She actually had an addiction to being critical and to being a victim. Her point of view was, "He's selfish, he's hurting me with his addiction, he's doing terrible things." Interestingly, when I asked my client to make a list of all the ways he had harmed his spouse, he was unable to come up with anything specific. He saw that when he bought her complaints as real, he affirmed her position as the aggrieved spouse and gave her additional opportunities to berate, accuse and diminish him.

As the man and I worked together, he became more aware of the dynamics of the situation and more willing to show up in his life and let go of his drug use. The happier, more creative and successful he became, the nastier the wife got until even her children didn't want to be around her. He eventually separated from her. The sad part is, she could have chosen to change and end her addiction, but she held on more and more tightly to being the critical, abusive victim she chose to be.

I encourage you to have a look at what's really going on with people who call you selfish. Is it about you? Or is it really about them? One of the ways to step into being the antidote to addiction is to ask yourself:

- Am I in the equation of my life here—or have I entered into somebody else's reality?

- Am I doing what other people want me to do with no regard for what I require?

If you are fitting yourself into someone else's reality, you cannot have your own. You cannot begin to restore the power of you to you and be who you truly are. And if the other person's reality is smaller than yours, you have to deny your awareness and contract yourself down enough to fit into their tiny life. I'm not saying that you shouldn't consider the effect your actions have on others. This is not about being a bull in a china shop. It's about seeing where you or others judge you as selfish when what you're doing is actually a contribution to and expansion of your life.

"You're Unpredictable"

Sometimes people are accused of being selfish when they're being unpredictable. If you're not doing the predictable thing that people count on you doing, they might accuse you of being self-centered. But you're not being self-centered; you're being present—and for many people, being present is one of the biggest sins, because when you're being present, they can't control you. You're apt to choose something that is not predictable because you're following the energy in the moment rather than operating on automatic pilot.

Let's say you have a set-in-stone plan for what you do on a Sunday. Then one Sunday morning, you wake up, and you're not looking forward to the plan. It feels heavy. Are you willing to ask, "What would feel fun and expansive today rather than going to a matinee movie, taking the kids to Chuck E. Cheese, or having brunch with the Joneses?" Maybe you would choose to take a hike or explore a park or stay home and play board games. Isn't being unpredictable what life is about? I don't mean making your unpredictability a chore for others. I mean being willing to follow the energy. Here's one of the funny things about addiction: Addiction makes you very, very predictable. Haven't you found that? "After lunch, I have a cigarette," "Five o'clock, cocktail time." "Date night, let's do porn on the Internet."

What if you were willing to be unpredictable in the sense of being you in the moment, being aware and asking questions like:

- What would be fun for me right now?
- What new or different activity could I choose today?
- What would expand my life?

If you were willing to be unpredictable, how much would your life change? How much more alive would you feel?

One aspect of being unpredictable is the willingness to change your mind. That's what you do when you're alert, aware and tuned in to yourself and what's going on around you. What if you were willing to change your mind every ten seconds? What if you didn't have to stick with something just because at one point you decided to do it?

Have you ever agreed to take a job, and you knew on the first day that it wasn't a good fit? But because you said you would take it on, you stayed for six years? Or maybe it was a marriage or a relationship. Did you decide you needed to stay forever even though you both were miserable? What if you allowed yourself to change your mind and not put yourself in the chains of sticking with something that wasn't working? Because, once again, when you do that, you are leaving yourself out of your life.

I'm not talking about totally disregarding others. I'm talking about being aware and honest with yourself about what's working and what's not working. You can ask questions like, "What would it take for this to be expansive for everyone?" It's about looking for possibilities—because we're all interconnected and there are ways in which you can totally be you and include the people who are willing to be in your life. If your marriage isn't working, does it really benefit your spouse and the kids to stay in it? Kids are aware of what's going on. I've had so many adult clients who have said things like, "I wish my parents had gotten a divorce. My life would have been so

Choice and Awareness

Most people think of choice as something they get to exercise when they're faced with different alternatives. They think they get to choose between vanilla ice cream or chocolate, they can choose to be married or divorced or they can choose to spend their vacation in Costa Rica, California, Hawaii or Canada. This is what I call choice from a menu. It presupposes that the set options or answers in front of you are the only choices you have.

As an example, let's take the statement, "You can be married—or you can be divorced." If you look at what most people mean by married, you can see how they get stuck in the idea that they only have two choices. But what if you didn't define marriage the way everyone else does? What if it didn't mean living together 365 days a year, playing out certain roles and settling into established routines and expectations of one another? What if it was about honoring the other person for who he or she truly was and being present with that person in the moment rather than having set ways of behaving and acting? What if staying married was a choice you made every day, not out of having to analyze things, but out of following the energy? Might that open you up to a different and more expansive relationship? There are always choices beyond the "menu" set forth by this society. It's the arbitrary judgments and rules we take on that limit our choices. Most of us are led to believe that we have limited options in any given situation, but that's generally not the case.

Here's another example. I talked with a client who said, "I'm an over-doer. When Christmas comes, I insist that we do all the traditional things—set up the tree, make a turkey dinner, bake cookies and buy gifts for everyone. I exhaust myself and end up forcing all of that on my kids, who don't really care about it. I don't want to do that any more—but I don't want to skip Christmas because I love it."

I said, "Why don't you sit down with your kids and have a family meeting? You could choose things you like to do together. If you want to celebrate Christmas on December 27th to miss all the fuss, do that. Or if you want to pile everyone in the car and take a road trip over the holidays, do that. Do something fun that works for all of you. You always have many more choices than you believe."

She said, "Oh! That is so much more freeing!"

True choice is moving beyond the options you've been told are the only ones you have. You always have more choices than you believe you have.

We Are Continuously Choosing

A mistake people commonly make is not recognizing that we're continuously making choices. We are choosing something every second of our lives. We're choosing to treat ourselves well—or not. We're choosing to connect with a person—or not. We're choosing to engage in our addictive or compulsive behavior—or not. We're choosing even if we choose to be unaware that we're choosing. If you're operating on automatic pilot, you're simply choosing to go on automatic pilot. If, every time you see a particular house or car or person, you automatically say, "Ugh!" you're choosing to re-enact the same judgment over and over again.

Choice Creates Awareness*

Few people understand that they increase their awareness through making choices. Many people try to become aware of what their choices will create before they choose. But it doesn't work that way. Choice creates awareness. Awareness does not create choice.

Have you ever gone out on a date with someone and almost immediately become aware of whether or not there was a future with that person? Your choice to date them created that awareness. Sometimes you can have the awareness just from the act of making the choice. You don't actually have to go forward with it. If you say, "I'm going to go back to school and complete my degree," you'll immediately get the energy of what that choice will create. Then you may make another choice, "Oh, well, maybe this is not the time."

Choosing is crucial for awareness. My suggestion is to keep choosing, choosing, choosing, which you're doing anyway, but to become aware of the fact that you're choosing.

---

*"Choice creates awareness" is an Access Consciousness® concept.

much easier if I hadn't been stuck in the middle of their fights." The same can be said for a job. If you hate your work, can you actually do a good job for your employer? Or would they be better off with someone who truly enjoyed the work?

Check In

I would like you to check in with yourself right now and see if you're still being the energy of expansion. If, for some reason, you slipped back into being more contracted, would you please take a moment right now and expand out again? When you're learning new information from the space of expansion, it's much easier to see what's true for you and what resonates with you than when trying to learn from a place of contraction.

Exercise: The Event Lie

One of the things that prevents us from being the antidote to our addictive behavior is the decisions, judgments and conclusions we have made about our past experiences and what we believe they say about us and the universe. Here's an exercise you can use to begin to work with this. I call this exercise, "The Event Lie."

Please pick one or two events from your childhood that still have a charge for you. They don't have to be huge things. I'm not talking about big events like a death in the family or a time you moved. It can be something that seems small—something that happened at school or when you were visiting your cousins. Not big abuse, just something that's still charged.

Here's an example from my own life. I was in second grade. It was October 31st, Halloween. I was very excited about dressing up in my costume and going around the neighborhood with the kids in my class to get goodies. We went to one house, and the woman had an enormous bowl of candy. She told us, "Take as much as you want." I was thrilled, so I reached in and took two or three handfuls of candy.

When we got back to the classroom, the teacher told everyone in the class that I and another boy, who had also taken a lot of candy, were greedy and didn't have manners. She made us as wrong as wrong could be. That stuck with me for a long time. And even as an adult, the incident had a charge for me. Every time I'd think of it, I would cringe. That's the kind of event I'm talking about.

As a result of that experience, I concluded that I was a bad girl, that I was greedy and that it was not right to engage in pleasurable things. In other words, I was wrong and I needed to contract. I also decided that I couldn't trust adults. Even though the lady invited me to take the candy, I was so humiliated by the teacher that I didn't want to trust what any adult said again. That's a lot of stuff to come out of one brief Halloween event when I was six or seven years old. And for years, I lived from those decisions, judgments and conclusions. They colored many of my responses to the events in my life.

Many years later when I went back and looked at those decisions, I realized that I wasn't greedy after all. The lady with the bowl of candy was gifting to me, and I was joyfully receiving her gift—until the teacher made me wrong. I had to look at the incident from a different perspective in order to understand that I was not the one who was wrong in this situation; it was that teacher. I finally was able to let go of the charge and say, "Wow, I made some inaccurate decisions, judgments and conclusions—and I allowed them to run my life. And all of those decisions contributed to my addictive behavior—because they all gave me the sense that I was wrong and couldn't trust myself or others."

When I did the Event Lie exercise with a friend, she remembered an incident that occurred when she was five years old. She had carefully selected her clothes and dressed herself, and she proudly went out to show her mom what a good job she had done. Guess what happened? Her mom ridiculed and shamed her. My friend felt humiliated and concluded that she couldn't trust herself to make good decisions.

When my friend went back and looked at the situation, she realized that it wasn't that she made bad choices; it was that her mom was mean. She had a mean mother—some of us do. She saw that she could actually make very good decisions, and she looked at some of the places in her life where she had done that but hadn't acknowledged it. She couldn't let go of her judgments about herself until she looked at the conclusion she made at age five. Nor could she let in the information that during her life, she had actually made some very good decisions.

Why is this exercise so powerful? It's because your point of view creates your reality.* If you conclude at age six or seven that you're greedy and you can't trust people, or if you conclude at age five that you make bad decisions, you will create circumstances that demonstrate the correctness of those conclusions—until you go back and look at them. We create lies for ourselves about the meaning of the events in our life. And these lies contribute to our sense of being wrong and play into the addictive or compulsive behavior we choose to engage in.

So, right now, I invite you to write down your event. Once again, it's an event from your childhood that may seem small, but that has a charge for you. Do you have one? Write down what happened for you.

After you've done that, please look at the decisions, judgments and conclusions you made about yourself, about life, other people, adults and maybe God or the universe, based on that incident. And write those down as well.

After you complete that part of the exercise, I encourage you to go back and look at yourself as the little boy or girl you were at that time, and ask yourself, "If I were standing outside of this situation

---

*"Your point of view creates your reality" is an Access Consciousness® concept.

and I saw these things happening to a child, what would I say to that child?" What is it that someone could have said to you at the time that would have put this incident in the right perspective for you? Please write that down.

I would like you to say that to yourself now. By saying it, you can correct the decisions, judgments and conclusions you made as a small child, which have shaped your point of view—and may still be influencing how you interact in the world. Spotting old lies, inaccurate decisions, judgments and conclusions is a big step in the process of uncovering the truth of who you really are.

Some Tools You Can Begin Using Now

Here are some questions and tools that will empower you to become more of you, which is what becoming the antidote to addiction is all about.

Tool: Is It Light—or Is It Heavy?*

I'd like to introduce a tool that I've found extremely valuable: *That which is true makes you feel light, and that which is a lie makes you feel heavy.*

This might help you to understand it better: Think of someone in your life you care about—someone you're willing to be with and have no judgment of. Get the energy of that. Is that heavy or light? My guess is that you feel a lightness in that.

Now get the energy of someone who has betrayed you or someone you thought was a friend until you realized he or she was not kind or friendly at all. Is there a heaviness in that? That's because there's a lie there. The lie was that person cared about you or was going to do what was in your best interest.

---

*"Is it light? Or is it heavy?" is an Access Consciousness® tool.

Each individual experiences *light* and *heavy* in a different way. Some people experience a sense of heaviness or a lightness in the body. Other people get the word—*heavy* or *light*. Some people experience light like day, and heavy like night. It doesn't matter how it shows up for you. Please don't judge that. This is not something you have to get right. It's a response that is unique for you, and once you become aware of what *light* and *heavy* are for you, it becomes an extremely valuable tool. I use it all the time to get clear about what is true for me and what's going on in my life. I also make use of it when I am making choices or considering different possibilities.

For example, if I'm looking at going on a trip or attending a particular class, even though logically it might seem like a good idea or a bad idea, I'll get the energy by asking something like, "What is the energy of attending this class or going on this trip?" There will be a heaviness or a lightness to it, and often the heavy or light energy counteracts what my logical mind would have figured out. I've noticed that when I follow the energy of what's light, things always work out well. And when I don't—when I follow my logical mind— things never work out in the positive way I think they're going to.

I want to add a caveat here. The only way the heavy/light tool works accurately is if you're willing to have no point of view about what the response or outcome is going to be. If you have already decided that something is good for you or bad for you, or that somebody is this way or that way, the heavy/light tool won't work. The energetic response to your question is going to agree with what you've already decided. For example, if you've decided that person "x" is the right person for you to marry and you ask, "Is it heavy or light for me to marry person 'x?'" you're going to get a *light*. The tool can't work because you already have a judgment in place.

If you want to ask about marrying person "x," you have to approach the question from a place of complete neutrality: "If it's expansive for me to marry person 'x,' great. If it's not expansive for me to marry person 'x,' great." It's only from a place of no expectations or desired results that the heavy/light tool will work.

You can use this tool when you feel drawn to engage in your addictive or compulsive behavior, by asking:

- What is the energy of engaging in my addictive or compulsive behavior right now?
- Is it heavy or light for me to put this behavior off for fifteen minutes?

Even if you find that it's heavy for you to engage in your addictive or compulsive behavior, you can still choose to do it. The purpose of the heavy/light tool is not to tell you what to do; it's simply to give you more awareness of what you're choosing.

Here are some additional ways you can use this tool with your addiction. Ask:

- Joe is supportive of me getting free of my addictive or compulsive behavior. Is that heavy or light?
- This (activity or idea) would contribute to me in letting go of my addictive or compulsive behavior. Is that heavy or light?

Once again, I'm talking about the lightness or the heaviness of the energy. As you begin to recognize and follow the lighter energy, you will begin to choose the things that will help you to be free from your addictive and compulsive behavior.

If you're anything like me, you have tried to figure things out by thinking them through. Please recognize, despite what you may have been told, that thinking doesn't work. And here's another thing about thinking: Every time you go into thinking and figuring something out, you're cutting off your awareness of what's going on. Thinking actually prevents you from being aware. You can do one or the other, you can be aware—or you can think—but you can't do both at the same time.

Thinking has gotten you where you are. If thinking could have gotten you out of your addictive or compulsive behavior, you'd be out of it by now. That's why this tool, which asks you to perceive the energy of the situation (rather than trying to think something through), is so effective.

You can use the light/heavy tool to access your knowing at any time. If it's light, it's true for you. It's not a universal truth; it's simply true *for you*. And if it's heavy, there's a lie there—spoken or unspoken. It's good to know that sometimes lies are unspoken. You have to look for those, too, because anything that's heavy is going to stick your attention until you spot the lie.

For instance, let's say someone tells you, "I can't come to your party today because I'm sick." You might say to yourself, "Hmm, that feels heavy to me. Is there a lie here? Yes. (That feels light.) Is she really sick? No. (That feels light). Oh, okay. I get it. She's not sick."

If you find that your questions don't lighten the energy up entirely, there might be more to the lie. You can ask:

- What else is there that's a lie?
- What's the unspoken lie here?
- What else is going on?

It may be something the person is not telling you like, "Well, actually, my spouse doesn't want me to go to your party because he's afraid I'm going to flirt with so-and-so." As soon as you get the unspoken lie, you can let it go. It will feel light. So this is a very practical and helpful tool.

Use the heavy and light tool as you go through your day. Notice what feels light and follow that light energy. Notice what feels heavy. Don't resist and react to the heaviness because that's fighting it, and fighting keeps you in it. Instead ask yourself, "What can I be and do to create a situation that's lighter here?" As you ask yourself that question, you'll get some kind of awareness. Just go in that direction.

Tool: Who Does This Belong To?*

Have you ever found yourself walking down the street, feeling quite happy with life, and all of a sudden, a wave of sorrow overcame you? Or perhaps you were sitting at home, watching a movie and you noticed you were very angry. Would it surprise you to know that many of your thoughts, feelings and emotions don't actually belong to you?

Many of us are incredibly psychic; I find this particularly with people who have addictive or compulsive behaviors. When I say "psychic," I'm not talking about reading tea leaves or looking into a crystal ball. I'm referring to our ability to pick up the thoughts, feelings and emotions of everyone around us. If you're aware of this as an ability you have, then it's not a problem. But if you're not aware that you pick up others' feelings and thoughts, you're going to assume that the sadness or anger or whatever it is, is yours, and that you need to do something about it. The thing is, if it's not yours to begin with, there's nothing you can do about it.

Here's an example: One Christmas, I went to the mall to do some Christmas shopping. I have a small family and I had plenty of money to cover the expense of the presents I was going to buy. When I came out of the mall, having made my purchases, I was thinking, "Oh my God! How am I ever going to pay for this? I don't know what to do about my credit cards." All of a sudden I realized it wasn't my thought! It was what many of the people in the mall were thinking as they were overspending and putting all their purchases on their credit cards. So, knowing that those thoughts weren't mine, I just let them go.

But for many people, it's not always so clear-cut, especially if they don't acknowledge that they have the ability to pick these things up.

---

*"Who Does This Belong To?" is an Access Consciousness® tool.

That's where this tool comes in. Any time you have a thought, feeling or emotion, ask, "Who does this belong to?" If it lightens up at all, it's not yours and you can say, "Return to sender."

As a therapist for many years, I've seen people who worked their anger issues for a decade without ever changing anything—because the anger wasn't theirs in the first place. They were picking it up from a parent, spouse, family member, or boss, and they were acting it out for them. Once they got that the anger wasn't theirs, it just went away.

It is also possible, if you are experiencing physical or emotional pain, that you're picking up other people's pain and taking it on as your own. This happens all the time. Ask the question, "Who does this belong to?" If it lightens up, you'll know you're picking it up from someone else, and you can return it to sender.

You can also use, "Who does this belong to" to deal with thoughts, feelings and emotions surrounding your addictive or compulsive behavior. For example, try using it with whatever thoughts, feelings or emotions come up when you're *considering* engaging in your addictive or compulsive behavior or when you *have* engaged in it.

I recommended this tool to a woman who had a problem with drinking. She would get anxious and uncomfortable and then turn to alcohol for some relief. I suggested that she ask, "Who does this belong to?" as soon as she became aware of the anxiety. She came into our next session smiling brightly. She discovered she was picking up *her husband's* anxiety, mistaking it as her own, and then taking a drink in order to feel more calm.

Tool: Ask Good Questions

Another useful and effective thing you can do to have and become more of you and to end your addictive or compulsive behavior is to consistently be in the question. Questions empower. They expand things energetically and they open you up to new possibilities. Any open-ended question will help you to start expanding when you feel contracted. Constantly asking questions rather than coming to conclusion, judgment and decision about your particular addictive or compulsive behavior (or anything else in your life) can open you to new avenues of awareness and action.

Many people think they are asking questions, when much of the time, their questions aren't real questions. They are answers with question marks on the end.

Here's an example of what I mean. Say you've decided that you want the man of your dreams to show up in your life, and he has to be tall, dark and handsome. You might ask a "question" like, "What is it going to take for the man of my dreams to show up next week?" That's not a real question. It's a statement of what you have decided you want with a question mark at the end. A true question is about something you haven't already made a decision about. A true question leaves the possibilities open.

You think you're asking for the man of your dreams, but since you've already decided what he has to look like, you've limited what the universe can gift to you. What if the man who would be the greatest contribution to your life is short and has blond hair? What if it takes a month for him to show up? The more requirements you put on your "question" the less likely anything will show up.

When I work with people and their addictions, sometimes they ask things like, "How do I stop my addictive or compulsive behavior?" That's not a real question either. It's a statement of a decision they've made (that they have to stop) with a question mark at the end. This approach leads to dealing with addiction in the fight mode. It also limits what can show up, because you've already decided what has to happen. A better question would be, "What's it going to take for this behavior to change?" because change can show up in all kinds of different ways. A question invites you to expand your awareness. It opens you up to new possibilities.

Some of the other questions you could ask about your addictive or compulsive behavior could be:*

- What else is going on here that I haven't been willing to be aware of?
- What else is possible here?
- How does it get any better than this?**
- What could I change here?
- What other actions could I take?
- What other energy could I be that would change this?

---

*A number of these questions are used throughout the book. They're some of the most valuable questions you can have in your repertoire.

**"How Does It Get any Better Than This?" is an Access Consciousness® tool.

CHAPTER THREE

What's Right About Addiction

All behavior is purposeful.
You would not be choosing an addictive or compulsive behavior
if it wasn't a contribution to your life in some way.

In this chapter, we're going to explore the question, "What's right about addiction?" I know that seems like a crazy question, and I'm going to talk about what makes it crucial for you to actually answer it.

Often addictive or compulsive behavior can seem like the best way to get many needs met, and it may have been the best coping mechanism you had at the time. In fact, many people use their addictive or compulsive behavior to meet a wide variety of needs. Once you begin to identify all the ways your addiction has helped you and been right for you, you can consider whether this is the way you desire to continue to get those needs met.

When I ask, "What's right about addiction?" most people look at me like I'm nuts. They say, "Addiction is terrible. It's horrible. It's the worst thing. It's what's stopping me from being me. I hate the alcohol. I hate the cigarettes. I hate the abusive relationships. I don't know why I keep choosing them."

I say, "Let me tell you something I learned long ago. All behavior is purposeful. You would not be choosing an addictive or compulsive behavior if it didn't do something for you. You wouldn't be choosing it if it wasn't a contribution to your life in some way. You created your addiction in the first place because you thought you didn't have any other choice. You didn't have the information, the tools or the skill set to choose something different. You had to create some kind of addictive or compulsive behavior in order deal with whatever was going on for you."

Being aware of that is an important step. But it's also somewhat paradoxical—because the other side of that contribution has been a limitation. And you have to look at both sides of the contribution/limitation to get free of addictive or compulsive behavior.

I recently began to work with a new client who had been abandoned and badly abused as a child. She said, "I'm an alcoholic."

I asked, "What does that mean?"

She said, "I drink almost every night."

I asked, "How much?"

She said, "About a bottle of wine. I drink because I just can't deal with the pain of seeing what a mess I've made of my life and how difficult things are."

I asked her, "Do you have gratitude for the drinking and the alcohol?"

She said, "No! Why would I have gratitude for that?"

I said, "Ask yourself, 'If I hadn't had the alcohol to deal with the pain of the abandonment, the abuse and the sense of wrongness, what would my life have been like?'"

She started to cry, and said, "I probably would have killed myself."

I asked, "Can you see what a gift the alcohol has been? That doesn't mean it is not time to change that, but it was a gift for you when you didn't have any other way of approaching things."

And the great thing is—she got it.

it's been amazing to me how many clients have discovered that their addicitive behavior has actully kept them alive until they could get real help. Please check and see if that has been true for you. Perhaps you will begin to see what a gift your addictive or compulsive behavior has actually been!

Now you are looking to move beyond your addictive or compulsive behavior, and it's going to be very helpful to discover the ways that behavior has served you. So, let's look at this question, "What's right about your addiction that you're not getting?" As a way of assisting you to do that, I'd like to talk about some of the responses I've gotten from my clients who were willing to look at what their addiction contributed to their lives.

It helps me to cope. It's my best stress reliever. Many people use their addictive or compulsive behavior as their primary way of dealing with stress. I often hear things like, "I can handle seeing my ex because I know that afterwards I can have a bottle of wine," or "I can deal with the kids because I know that later I can retreat into my office and relax by playing computer games for a couple of hours."

If you don't have good, practical tools to deal with your stress, your addictive or compulsive behavior can seem like a lifesaver. The difficulty is that in the end, you're making yourself dependent on it and diminishing your awareness and capacity to deal with stress in a way that's more productive for you.

It relieves emotional or physical pain. If you have emotional or physical pain that you can't seem to manage any other way, it makes sense that you would turn to an addictive or compulsive behavior to relieve it—because the whole point of addiction is to not be aware and present with you. It's a way for you to not exist, at least temporarily, and in that state of diminished awareness, you get some relief.

However, both emotional and physical pain are signs that there's something you need to be aware of. So, when you're using your addictive or compulsive behavior to relieve that pain, you're putting your awareness on hold. That can be okay for a while; however, in some cases, there are things you will need to take care of based on that awareness and if you don't take care of it, it could be damaging to you.

It helps me feel more at ease in social situations. Maybe having a cocktail or smoking a joint helps you feel at ease socially, so you interact with people more comfortably. Maybe the pain medication you take to help you get a good night's sleep enables you to go out and enjoy people more. Or maybe looking for what's wrong in people's lives and fixing their problems relaxes you and allows you to feel that you are being of service.

While all of that seems to make sense, when you're using an addictive or compulsive behavior to help you feel more at ease, you cut off the possibility of using the tools or developing the skills that will allow you to feel comfortable without the addictive behavior.

It stops the mind chatter. Have you ever had the sense that you have a committee in your head? That every time you tried to make a decision, there's one voice saying *this* and another voice saying *that*? Many people use their addictive or compulsive behavior to stop that kind of mind chatter. It seems to quiet the mind and turn down the volume on the contradictory voices.

But if that's the only way you have to stop the mind chatter, you make yourself dependent on your addictive or compulsive behavior rather than having choice in how you would like to handle it.

It helps me receive. Receiving is about dropping your barriers, opening yourself up and allowing someone or something to contribute to you. Some people have had life experiences that were so painful that they decided they could not trust others or that the universe was against them. Their way of staying "safe" has been to cut off their receiving from anyone or anything other than their addiction. They will tell you that they receive love, care, comfort, support or relaxation only when they are engaging in their addictive or compulsive behavior.

If you've had difficult, abusive experiences, you too may have come to the conclusion that it's too dangerous to open yourself up and receive from anybody or anything except your addiction. This is a common, totally understandable conclusion, based on the experiences you have had.

Unfortunately, whatever receiving you are excluding from your life right now is part of what is keeping you in the contracted energy of addiction, because your addictive or compulsive behavior is always about limiting your possibilities. Making the decision that you won't receive from anyone or anything except your addictive or compulsive behavior is like deciding you will only shop in your neighborhood convenience store for everything you need in your life. As you begin to trust yourself to know what you know, you will find it easier to receive from sources other than your addictive or compulsive behavior.

It cuts off my awareness. It can seem like a great relief to have your awareness cut off. You don't have to deal with whatever it is you're aware of. You don't have to know what to do or how to handle it. If there are problems in your marriage, if you have financial or legal difficulties, if a family member is abusing you or if the pain of not fitting in anywhere seems overwhelming, then cutting off your awareness may seem like the only possible solution—and you can definitely use your addictive behavior to do that.

Unfortunately, you can't cut off your awareness of one thing without cutting off your awareness of everything, so you can end up blocking your awareness of people and situations that might be harmful to you. That's one of the reasons many people with addictions find themselves in abusive situations. You might cut off your awareness of someone who is going to betray you, steal from you, batter you or in any other way, abuse and limit you.

Gifting and Receiving*

Most of us are taught that life on this planet is about give-and-take, tit-for-tat. It's about keeping score, so if I do something for you, you should do something for me. We deny the awareness that a person giving a gift receives through the giving. And a person who receives a gift gives through receiving. This is called the simultaneity of giving and receiving.

What if, when someone gave you any kind of gift, it was done in the spirit of true giving? Not many people operate from that space, but a few do. What if you could allow yourself to have and be the energy of receiving that gift, rather than automatically going into, "They gave me a $75 gift, now I have to give them a $75 gift. I have to make sure the score is even"? That idea limits you in so many ways.

One of the biggest ways the idea of give-and-take limits you is that it restricts your ability to receive what is gifted. If you assume that everything anyone gives you is going to cost you, it's going to be very hard to move out of your addictive or compulsive behavior, because your addiction is also based on the false idea of give-and-take. You've decided that your addiction gives you something—comfort or relief from not fitting in or whatever it is for you—and at the same time, you also know that it costs you. It may cost you your relationship or your job. It may cost you your self-respect and it may be a huge distraction from your life. When you're involved in the give-and-take-reality of addiction, you think that in order to have peace, relief, comfort and anything positive in your life, you have to pay dearly for it. However, once you move beyond the give-and-take reality into the awareness of oneness, you can have and be it all without it "costing" you anything.

If you allow yourself to move into the energy of gifting and receiving, you can receive from everything—because everything is conscious. You can receive from trees, you can receive from animals and you can receive from

*"Gifting and Receiving" is an Access Consciousness® concept.

the people around you. Can you get the idea of how being open to this kind of receiving would expand you and your world—and simultaneously diminish the power of your addiction?

As contrary as it might seem, your willingness to receive also creates you as the gift. Have you ever had the experience of giving someone a present that you knew was just the right thing for them and feeling so wonderful when they received it? You gifted the present and simultaneously received the other person's joy in receiving it. And in the process of receiving, that person became a gift to you.

Pets often provide a great example of what gifting and receiving looks like. They gift to you simply because they can, and they receive your gifts without considering what they need to do to "repay" you. That's what I would like you to begin to do as well. As you begin to receive from everything, from the sky and the sunshine to the couch you're sitting on, the buildings around you and even the pavement, you will begin to see that your addictive or compulsive behavior is not the only thing that can gift you what you're looking for. In a similar way, art, literature, music and many other things can be incredible gifts for you. Looking at a painting or reading a book is also a contribution to the book or painting. Once again, it's about the simultaneity of gifting and receiving.

There's one other important point about give-and-take, and another reason to move out of that way of operating. Give-and-take is based on judgment. If you're judging what you have to do or what you need to give back in return for a gift, you cannot be in the relaxed energy of receiving. This is a way that judgment destroys what's possible for you. Please let go of the judgment associated with give-and-take. When you begin to move towards gifting and receiving energy, you will find greater ease with any addictive or compulsive behavior because you will be willing to receive from everyone and everything in the entire universe rather than limiting your receiving to your addictive or compulsive behavior.

You can also cut off your awareness of everything that would like to gift to you—the universe, the Earth, certain people and animals—so you're stuck with a very limited, often barren reality.

I've been talking about cutting off your awareness because that's what we *appear* to do when we engage in our addictive or compulsive behavior. For many of us, that's the whole purpose of the behavior. However, this is a case of appearances only. When we are engaging in any addictive or compulsive behavior, we actually are receiving all that we could be aware of, and sometimes, particularly with alcohol or drugs, we are exponentializing those awarenesses. The difficulty is that these awarenesses get stored in the sensory cortex and are then not available to us. Unfortunately, they can still affect us, which is why we sometimes experience odd, illogical, seemingly out-of-the-blue reactions to certain people and/or situations.

It allows me to continue being a victim. There's something to be said about being a victim. For example, when you're a victim, you don't have to be responsible for your life. You don't have to step up, make a demand or take action. You can be passive and inactive. You can take comfort in knowing that whatever is going on in your life has to do with someone or something other than you. You don't have to be wrong.

Your life may have felt overwhelming to you because no one ever gave you the tools, information or coping skills that would allow you to handle it more easily. You can't seem to create a life that works for you. When that's the way life seems, choosing to be a victim gives you a little bit of relief. You can say, "Well, I'm the victim of the economy, my childhood abuse, my genes, my addiction or whatever it is, so I'm not responsible for it." I totally get that. When you're a victim, you don't have to deal with those difficult things.

But does being a victim actually work for you? Is it actually real and true for you? I invite you to use the heavy/light tool with this. Say aloud, "I'm a victim of my addiction or my life" or whatever it is that you've decided you're the victim of. Is that heavy or light?

Every time I say that to myself, it's so heavy I practically sink into the ground. But please say it for yourself. You know what you know.

Being a victim may have been the best choice you had for coping with life at one time, but being a victim is a guarantee that you will never step into being who you truly are. It dooms you to a small, contracted life.

It makes me feel safe. People often tell me the only time they feel safe is when they are engaging in their addictive behavior. They're kind of like kids who build a fort out of tablecloths and hide there with their teddy bear and the idea that no one can "get" them. You may have done something like that. You may have hidden under the bed or tried to hide your body in some other way. Or you may have just hidden *you,* which is what a lot of us have done. We hide who we are—that's part of the process of cutting off the parts and pieces of ourselves.

Staying small is a way of hiding out and looking for a way to stay safe. It's pretty scary to step into who you truly are when you've been diminished, punished or made wrong for being you. Something that provides you with a sense of safety or a place of refuge—and that may be your addiction—seems like a positive thing.

Often people choose addiction because it helps them to feel safe by not being present. Not being present in our life gives us the illusion that nothing bad can happen to us—or even if it does, we won't be aware enough to have to deal with the full force of the experience. Unfortunately, not being present actually makes you more likely to be the victim of someone or something because you cut off your awareness of potentially dangerous situations. You lock yourself into a kind of oblivion where you are apt to be blindsided.

The only real safety is in your willingness to be totally aware and to receive everything that's going on around you, including everything your body is trying to tell you. It sounds counter-intuitive, yet it is true. *Safety comes from the willingness to be present and aware.*

It lets me punish myself for being wrong. If you've decided that you're wrong, it makes a lot of sense to punish yourself. For one thing, it gives you the sense that you're right by recognizing that you're wrong and punishing yourself. People with addictions often find a way to be right by being wrong.

And being wrong helps you to fit into this society. Everybody's happy for you to be wrong—because then you're like they are, and you are controllable. Being wrong is also a way that many people think they will find safety. They've decided they're less of a target if they're wrong. Actually, the opposite is true, because when you decide that you're wrong, you put up an energetic sign that says you're weak and vulnerable—and you're actually more likely to be a target.

Not long ago, I started working with a woman who told me she had an addiction to cocaine. In our first session, I asked her what she liked to do. She replied that she loved to paint, but that she hadn't allowed herself to buy any painting materials for months because she was punishing herself for having spent so much money on cocaine. The first thing I asked her to do was to go out and buy the materials she needed and begin to paint again. She did that and reported that when she lifted the punishment and began to treat herself well, she immediately started to lose interest in the cocaine.

Punishing ourselves is a self-perpetuating cycle. We punish ourselves for being wrong, which leads us to so much pain that we choose addiction, so we punish ourselves for having the addiction and then we use the addiction to punish ourselves for being wrong.

It's a way to hold my family system in place. I talked about this in chapter one. Your family may need for you to have an addictive or compulsive behavior in order to maintain the status quo in the family. Many families require a scapegoat. It's the person everyone else can point to as the source of the family's difficulties. Having a scapegoat allows people to feel good about themselves. They don't have to look at their own issues. Mom doesn't have to see how critical she is, Dad doesn't have to deal with his rage, Sister doesn't have to look at her eating disorder, and no one has to deal with the fact that Grandpa Joe seems overly interested in roughhousing with the children. The person who has chosen the addiction, particularly if it's alcohol or drugs, is often put in the role of being the scapegoat.

Every scapegoat knows, at some level, that if they stop their addictive behavior, the entire family system will either fall apart or the family will turn on them. I've seen it happen both ways. You may think you are being of service to the family in maintaining the energetic and emotional status quo. You may see this as a contribution to them. You know that you can tolerate being the problem or the scapegoat, but you don't know whether your family members can face their own problems.

As credible as this may sound, if you maintain your addiction (and the status quo in your family), you will never be able to be the gift to the world that you actually are. If the above is representative of your family, everyone in it is living a lie and that can't actually lead to anything good for anyone.

Moving Beyond the Judgment That Your Addiction Is Bad and Terrible

Can you begin to see some of the ways your addictive or compulsive behavior has contributed to you? Until you are willing to look at what's right about your addiction, you will never be able to clear it. You will never be able to move beyond that behavior because you're operating out of the lie that it has not contributed anything to your life. Your addictive or compulsive behavior has actually been a contribution to you. It may not have been the best way of getting your needs met, but if you can think of it as the best tool you had at the time, you can begin to replace it with other tools—and move beyond it.

Acknowledging what's right about your addiction is an essential part of what allows you to move forward. Once you acknowledge all of the things it has done for you, whether it has been about coping with stress, relieving pain, providing comfort or a sense of ease and safety, you can begin to find different ways of meeting those needs.

Exercise:
What's Right About Your Addiction That You're Not Getting?

So, right now, please write down all the things that are right about your addictive or compulsive behavior and all the ways it has contributed to your life.

As you do this exercise, you may come up with some responses that seem embarrassing, strange or irrational. Please don't ignore those. Write down whatever comes up. There will be something important to discover about those answers, too. After you've written down all your answers, look over your list. What have you learned about your addictive or compulsive behavior? Write that down as well.

Taking the Exercise Further...Some Things You Can Do

At this point you may be thinking, "I get that there are some things that are right about my addiction, but how does that change anything?"

Here are a few things you can do right now to take the next steps for change.

Find a Little Gratitude

Now that you've written down all the things that are right about your addiction, see if you can find gratitude for the things it has done for you when you haven't had another way of fulfilling your needs, wants and desires. We all desire comfort and ease, a sense of peace and safety, a way to deal with stress and a sense that things can be right with the world. If your addiction was the only place you could find that until now, it has served a positive purpose in your life. It has served as a stopgap until you could find another way to fulfill those needs and desires. Be grateful for that.

Ask: What Else Could I Put into Place to Meet This Need?

I invite you to consider other ways of fulfilling the needs and desires, that until now, your addiction has satisfied. For instance, if you've discovered that your addictive or compulsive behavior has been the only way you were willing to receive comfort, begin to look for other ways of having that. You might find yourself jumping at the first answer as the solution. That's fine, but keep asking the question because there are always going to be more ways of providing yourself with a sense of well being and ease.

If shopping has given you sense of comfort, your first response might be to look for another addictive behavior that would provide that. See if you can come up with other ways of getting the relaxation and relief you desire. It might come from opening up to a real friend, receiving from an animal or giving yourself the pleasure of a long walk in nature, a hot bubble bath, or a massage. Keep asking questions about what else might work for you. Remember, you're not looking for one answer to solve it all. What gives you comfort one day may be different from what provides you with comfort the next.

Or say you've discovered that one of the big things your addictive or compulsive behavior has given you is relief from stress. What other things might you do to relieve stress? Could you take a jog, go for a swim, have a cup of tea or take a break from what you are doing? Even something like the Event Lie exercise can be a stress reliever because a great deal of stress is based on lies that come from the decisions, judgments and conclusions you've made.

Here's an interesting note about stress: Sometimes we're told a situation should be stressful, so we manufacture stress in order to go along with the way we think we're supposed to respond to it. For instance, having a loved one die is stressful for many people, but for others it isn't. It could be a relief; they might find a sense of peace in it. Yet, they may not allow themselves to have their own response to their loved one's death. They may manufacture the stress they think they're supposed to have. They may also take on the stress of everyone around them.

If you have a stressful response to any situation, you might ask, "Who does this stress belong to?" and "Am I responding in a way that I've decided I'm supposed to respond rather than in a way that's actually true for me?"

Ask: Is This Need Actually a Truth—or Is It a Lie?

Occasionally something that is masquerading as a need is actually a lie. For instance, let's say you're using your addictive behavior to help you stay a victim. You don't need to find another way to be a victim. It's much more helpful to recognize that being a victim is not the truth of who you are.

Another example of a lie could be the need to punish yourself for being wrong. If you let go of the punishing and treat yourself with kindness and caring, you will probably find it goes a long way in assisting you to move away from the addictive or compulsive behavior.

So, in addition to asking, "What else could I put in place to take care of this need?" you can go through your list of things that are right about your addiction and ask the question, "Is this need actually a truth—or is it a lie?" If it's a lie, just acknowledge it and let it go. You won't need to address it again. I encourage you to ask yourself these questions daily because every time you do, you're going to shift your awareness. And don't forget to use the light/heavy tool!

I highly recommend that you write down your answers every time you ask these questions. In this way, you will see how you are creating change.

CHAPTER FOUR

End Judgment, End Addiction

Judgment is a cornerstone for all societies—
and it's a huge part of what holds your addiction in place.

In this chapter, I'm going to talk about judgment and its relationship to addiction.

You might ask, "Judgment? What does judgment have to do
with addiction?"

The answer is, "Absolutely everything."

You might also ask, "What you do mean when you say, "End
judgment, end addiction? You make it sound like it's easy."

The truth is that for many people, ending judgment is neither
easy nor simple. Judgment forms the foundation of all societies and
cultures. From the time we're very young, we're taught, "This is
right," "That's wrong," "You're a good boy or girl," "You're a bad boy
or girl." These kinds of judgments follow us throughout our lives.
There's a way we're supposed to look, a way we're not supposed to
look, a way we're supposed to talk, a way we're not supposed to talk,
things we're supposed to do, things we're not supposed to do. And
that's just the beginning of the ways judgment permeates our lives.

As we grow up, judgment takes on more varied and diverse
forms. We encounter judgment from our family, our friends, our

culture, our religion, our colleagues, our bosses and our neighbors. Often we align and agree with these judgments and try to fit ourselves into what we are told is "right" so we can play the game like everyone else. And in the process, we diminish ourselves. We're rarely aware that we've done it—because it's not always easy to recognize judgments for what they are. Sometimes they can be very subtle.

Or perhaps we don't align and agree with the judgments that get delivered at us. Some of us go into resistance and reaction to the judgment and rebel against it. We actively try not to do what's "right" and instead we try to fit ourselves into roles and behaviors that are not socially acceptable. But either way, whether we align and agree or resist and react, we attach ourselves to that judgment, make it significant and in the process, we lose part of ourselves.

What's the Difference Between Judgment and Awareness?

It may help to clarify what judgment is if I contrast it with awareness. I can say, "It's a beautiful day," or "That dog looks sick," and you might wonder whether I am expressing a judgment or an awareness. That's because I can say the same words with judgment—or with awareness. So, how can you tell them apart?

When you express an awareness, there is no energetic charge. You don't have a sense within you of "good" or "bad." You're simply acknowledging what is. When you express a judgment, there is a charge. You get a feeling from the statement. It can be a positive or a negative feeling, but in either case, it's generally a strong feeling.

Judgment Is Always Arbitrary

There's another key point about judgment. It has nothing to do with what's true or real. It is always based on an arbitrary point of view. It's a personal bias, belief or opinion. A hundred years ago, many people in America went along with the statement, "Spare the rod and spoil the child." In other words, if you didn't beat your kid, you weren't being a good parent. It was a judgment. Nowadays those people would be arrested for child abuse. What was the judgment that children should be beaten based on? Nothing! It was just an arbitrary idea people went into agreement with.

Around that same time in America, women didn't have the right to vote. People of color and minority ethnic groups didn't have the same rights as everyone else. All of those people were judged—and sometimes they still are—as being less-than, wrong, deviant or unworthy. Once again, all of that is arbitrary. Judgments are never about truth—but we buy them as if they are. And because they're accepted by almost everyone around us, they're often difficult to recognize for what they are.

I grew up in an academic family in the northeast of the U.S., which is oriented around its grand, old academic institutions like Princeton, Harvard and Yale. My father was a professor and scientist at one of those universities. There were a lot of judgments in our family and our town that the only thing that mattered was your I.Q. score and the academic achievements you attained. It was commonly believed that only people who were not up to par intellectually would engage in business. No one would go into business unless they couldn't make it in the academic world—because being an academic was the only worthwhile thing to do. There was absolutely no allowance for people to pursue their unique interests, talents and abilities.

It was incredibly narrow, and needless to say, I picked up heaps of judgments about the whole academic thing, but I didn't see that until I moved across the country to Texas, which had some equally narrow, contracted and uniform judgments—but in a totally different way. Few people in Texas cared about your scholastic aptitude test scores or where you went to school. For many, it was all about sports. Often an entire town would turn out for a high school football game. That's what they cared about. For them, that's what was valuable, correct and significant. And if you were a female, it was about being flashy. Texas is an "if you've got it, flaunt it" state.

Neither the judgments of the people in the Northeast nor the judgments of people in Texas encouraged individuals to identify and develop their own unique talents and abilities and to go in whatever direction their interests led them. I'm not saying there aren't people in these areas who don't go against the accepted judgments of what's valuable or correct; however, many people receive negative judgments for the choices they make because they counteract what the majority has decided is important.

We buy judgments as true and real to the degree that we do not ask questions and become aware of other possibilities. If the society says the most important priority should be family, then it's difficult for individuals who, by nature, are entrepreneurial or artistic to feel free to make their art or their business the priority in their lives.

It takes concentrated effort to ferret out the judgments that we have bought. Judgments are sometimes so deeply engrained and pervasive that they're almost undetectable—until you actively start looking.

Exercise: What Unrecognized Judgments Have You Bought?

Here's an exercise you can do to begin to discover unrecognized judgments you may have taken on. Using the categories and questions given below, write down some of the judgments you have picked up from your culture, your family of origin, the place where you lived or the part of the country you grew up in. I call this your inheritance. Ask yourself questions like:

- What did my family (or the people around me) believe or judge about:

  Rich people   Poor people
  Women   Men

Politics	Religion
Money	Education
Marriage	Raising children
Food	Bodies
Addiction	The most important thing in life

- Am I still carrying any of these belief systems as my own?
- Are those beliefs and judgments true for me?

The things we experience and the things we're taught and told as we are growing up often don't seem strange, inaccurate or outrageous to us, even if they are. They seem normal, because that's what we're used to. It's what we know. Doing this exercise can give you an enormous amount of freedom because it is easy to misidentify and misapply as true the judgments you pick up as a child. If you buy those judgments as true and they don't resonate for you, then you have to begin making yourself wrong, and that goes a long way toward creating addictive or compulsive behavior.

Exercise: A Time When You Were Judged

Here's another exercise to do with judgment. In this exercise, I'm going to ask you to remember two different times when you were judged, and then I'm going to ask you to have a look at the energy of those judgments and any decisions you may have made about yourself in response to them.

A Time You Were Judged as Wrong

The first step is to think of a time when you were judged as wrong.

I did this exercise with a client I will call Barbara. She remembered a time when she was about nine years old. She was camping with her family in Glacier National Park. One rainy day, her parents took her to a place that sold groceries, hot dogs, and hamburgers, and the family spent several hours there. Barbara thought that was just fine. She was running around, talking to everybody and having a great time. At some point, she noticed that her parents were trying to corral her—but she didn't get it. Her point of view was, "This is fun. Why isn't everybody running around and laughing?"

When they got back to their campsite, Barbara's parents scolded her for being noisy and bothering other people. This was one of many incidents Barbara recalled in which she had been harshly judged and made wrong for being exuberant, and eventually she bought into those judgments and cut off that part of who she was. She became more serious and stopped herself every time she felt high-spirited and cheerful.

When Barbara first recalled the camping trip, it had a very heavy feeling for her. She saw that she had bought her parents' judgment (and the lie contained within in it that she was wrong) and began a process of shutting down her outgoing nature and her interest in other people. Spotting the truth of that judgment lightened things up for her.

Now, think of a time when you were judged as wrong, and write down the answers to the following questions:

- What had you done—or not done?
- Where were you?
- What was said or done to let you know you were being judged?
- Did you take on the judgment as if it were true?
- Did you align and agree with the judgment or did you resist and react to it?
- Did you judge yourself in some way?
- Did you then change yourself in some way?
- Did you diminish yourself?

A Time When You Were Judged in a Positive Way

The second step of this exercise is to think of a time when you were judged in a positive way. Many people see positive judgment as a good thing, but that's not always the case. It can also be very limiting. A judgment is a judgment is a judgment.

Here's an example that illustrates my point. When I was about ten years old, I brought home a report card with all A's, and my parents said, "How great you are! How smart you are! What a good worker you are!"

My reaction was, "Wow, if I want more of that praise, I'd better make sure I please everyone and do whatever my teachers say, so I get A's."

By choosing to please the teachers so I could get more of the praise and positive judgment I desired, I cut off the awareness that some of my teachers were, frankly, idiots and that I was not honoring myself when I did everything they said I should do and tried to be everything they said I should be.

Here's another example of the way in which a positive judgment can be limiting. Currently I'm working with a client who is stunningly gorgeous. She's also creative and kind. She works well with animals, she writes beautifully and she has artistic talents. But because her good looks were the only thing she was validated for, she has cut off her awareness of all the other parts of who she is. She has spent an enormous amount of time making sure that everything about her appearance is perfect. That became her focus in life. She hasn't appreciated or developed the parts of her that weren't judged positively. We're working on it, but she still doesn't get what an amazing being she is beyond her appearance.

Now, think of a time when you received a positive judgment from your parents or another authority figure, and write down your answers to these questions:

- What about you was being judged positively?
- What was the judgment you were given?
- Who gave it to you?
- Did you align and agree with the judgment or did you resist and react to it?
- What did you decide about yourself as a result of the judgment?
- Has that decision diminished or limited you in any way?

The Energy of Judgment/The Energy of Addiction

Judgments, both positive and negative, prepare us to make the choices that lead to addiction. That's because they cut off our awareness of who we actually are and what's possible for us. Every time we accept a judgment about ourselves as true, we diminish ourselves. We become limited by the judgment. If we're told that we're beautiful or smart or stupid, and we buy that, that's all we can identify ourselves as. We may also be a whiz at math or a gifted writer. We may be devilishly funny or incredibly intuitive, but those things get dropped out of the way we see ourselves. Judgment tends to view people in black-and-white and put them into small boxes. It reduces us, as the complex and multi-faceted beings we are, down to a few words. When we buy the judgment, we buy into a view of ourselves as less than we truly are. And that becomes our reality.

Remember the client who was obsessed about her appearance? She came to see me because she was concerned about her drinking. Until she is able to move into seeing herself more accurately, the alcohol will remain a problem. When we cut ourselves down that much, we require some form of addictive or compulsive behavior to deal with the pain.

Judgment leads us toward addiction because it takes us away from what we actually know to be true about ourselves. We don't actually allow ourselves to exist as the beings we are. It's like we become a cartoon or oversimplified line drawing version of ourselves. And from this point, it's very easy to move into the energy of addiction, which is also a place where we don't exist.

Judging Yourself and Your Addictive or Compulsive Behavior

The energy of addiction and the energy of judgment work together in another way as well. As you engage in addictive or compulsive behavior, you will probably begin to judge yourself in any number of ways, including things like, "I don't handle life well. I should be able to stop this behavior. I'm weak. I'm hurting everyone who cares about me."

People believe that judging their addictive or compulsive behavior helps to keep it under control. Actually the opposite is true. Judging your behavior only strengthens it. It becomes a self-perpetuating cycle: self-judgment leads to addictive or compulsive behavior, and the addictive or compulsive behavior leads to self-judgment—and on and on.

I know it sounds contrary to what you would expect, but if you give up your judgment of your addictive or compulsive behavior, you create a space where it can change. Have you ever noticed that when you try to control a person or a situation, that it's very hard on you—and the person or the situation doesn't want to budge? But if you let go of the control, you open things up and change can occur because you're not so invested in an outcome. You're not thinking, "I have to do this. I have to have this outcome." And really, that's just another judgment. It has nothing to do with being aware.

Move From Judgment into Awareness

What you can do is stop being invested in the outcome. Move from judgment to awareness. The more you're able to do that, the easier it's going to be to walk away from your addictive or compul-

85

sive behavior. I recently worked with a man who told me he had a real problem with gambling. He was trying to stop gambling completely. He said, "Every time I go out in the evening, I have the urge to place a bet. I keep thinking, "I have to place a bet, I have to place a bet. I can't stop thinking about it. It ruins my evening."

I asked him, "What would it be like if you didn't judge your desire to place a bet? What if you just went ahead and did it with total awareness?"

He said, "Well, I don't know. I'd probably keep placing one bet after another."

I said, "The next time you go out, why don't you place a bet—and don't judge yourself? Don't make judgments based on the past about what's going to happen if you place one bet. Just place a bet, be present with it, be aware and see what happens next."

He came back the next week and said, "Over the weekend, I went to the races with some friends. I placed a bet, and I didn't judge myself for it. I realized I didn't even want to place another. I was betting just to be part of the gang. I didn't even really enjoy it. It was fantastic!"

His choice to be aware rather than to judge created a completely different outcome for him.

Judgment Excludes Awareness

Judgment is always about excluding things. You're saying, "This is right. This is wrong and I won't have the wrongness or badness in my life." Exclusion creates a distorted view of what's actually going on. And it may be that something you've judged as bad and wrong could actually be a huge contribution to your life—but it's never able to be that contribution because you've excluded it.

I'll give you an extreme example of what I mean by exclusion. Recently I watched a show on TV about the Neo-Nazi movement in America. It's a small movement of people who believe that only straight, white people should be allowed to live in the United States. They attack and harass Jews, African Americans, homosexuals, Asian Americans, Latinos, Arab Americans, Native Americans and anyone with different religious or political views. Because of the way they exclude with their judgments, the Neo-Nazis prevent themselves from being aware of all of the amazing diversity and contribution these groups have to offer. Their world is very contracted, limited and barren.

Often when I talk about not excluding anything, people say, "But Marilyn, there are some truly awful things I definitely do not want in my life! For example, I don't want those crazy Neo-Nazis anywhere near me!"

I'd like to make an important point here. Not excluding doesn't mean you have to choose everything. It means you don't exclude things from your awareness. My universe includes those Neo-Nazis, but I don't choose their way. I do, however, choose the awareness that they exist. Not excluding them from my awareness makes me less apt to be the effect of their kind of thinking. I'm aware of Neo-Nazism *and* I'm not choosing it.

Excluding things puts you in a place where you're vulnerable— because you've excluded certain ideas, beings, events and possibilities. When you exclude things, you don't prevent them from having an effect on you. All you do is exclude the *awareness* that would let you know those things were going to impact you.

When you exclude something you can be broadsided by it. For example, the statement, "I live in a perfectly safe neighborhood. Nothing could ever happen to me here," is a judgment. One day you go out and you get mugged, and then you ask, "How did that happen?" The mugging didn't just *happen;* you *created* the possibility that it could occur when you shut off your awareness. You judged

The Access Consciousness Clearing Statement®

As I began to use the tools of Access Consciousness® in my work with clients who presented with addictions, I noticed that they began to get better faster. Part of that was the nature of the tools. For example, once you get the idea of, "Who does this belong to?" and you know that most of your thoughts, feelings and emotions don't belong to you, it frees up a lot of energy you were using to try to fix something that wasn't yours in the first place. And once you get the hang of heavy and light, you don't waste as much time trying to figure things out.

One of the tools that changes things most dramatically for people is the Access Consciousness® clearing statement. Let me briefly describe how it works. When I ask you a question—or when you ask yourself a question—it brings up an energy. For instance, if I ask, "What was your family life like when you were a kid?" you'll notice an energy comes up. You don't need to put words to the energy. You can just be aware of it and allow it to be there. Often the energies that come up are contracted because they represent the judgments you've made about yourself and the events in your life. It's very helpful to clear them. This is a good point to use the Access Consciousness® clearing statement:

Everything that is times a godzillion, will you destroy and uncreate it all? Right and wrong, good and bad, POD and POC, all 9, shorts, boys and beyonds.®

The clearing statement is basically short-speak that allows you to clear away energy so you can move forward. Dr. Dain Heer of Access Consciousness® once described it as a cosmic vacuum cleaner. It goes "slooooop" and all the limitations that energy represents go away.

The clearing statement is an incredibly valuable tool when you're dealing with addiction. If you would like more information about it, please go to www.theclearingstatement.com/

that you lived in a perfectly safe neighborhood and you excluded the *awareness* that there could be a difficulty. I'm not talking about becoming paranoid. It's about empowering yourself to know what you know through being aware rather than cutting off your awareness with judgment.

Here's another example that may help you to understand exclusion: Imagine going into a grocery store. As you walk down the aisles, everything in the store is included in your awareness. You can see it all in technicolor. You're clearly not going to buy everything in the store, but you see it all. That's inclusion—that's awareness. Exclusion would be putting on blinders that keep you from seeing all the things you decided you didn't like or weren't going to buy. Those things would still be there, but they would not be visible to you. Do you see how that would limit your awareness? There might actually be something there you'd choose to add to your cart if you hadn't cut it out as a possibility.

Please don't exclude. And know that including everything in your awareness doesn't mean you have to *choose* it. It simply means that you're *aware* of its existence. And isn't it always better to be aware?

When you move out of judgment and exclusion and into awareness and question, you can begin to change things and shift the energy. That's what we're looking at doing—moving the energy, getting it out of the stuck, contractive place of addiction and the stuck, contractive places of judgment, which are pretty much one and the same.*

---

*In this chapter, I have talked about some of the more common ways that judgment shows up in relation to addiction. Judgment also takes many less-obvious forms, and if you're choosing to let go of judgment, it will be helpful to identify many of the more subtle ways judgment appears in your life. Additional information about these different forms of judgment can be found in the Appendix at the end of the book.

Judgment is such a huge subject that I'm going to talk about it in the next chapter as well. We'll look at a destructive form of self-judgment that people with addictions engage in and how you can begin to come out of the insanity of judging yourself, your life, and your behavior—and move into a place of greater awareness and possibility.

CHAPTER FIVE

The Primary Addiction: Judgment of the Wrongness of You

Underneath every addiction to alcohol, sex or whatever it is for you, lurks the primary addiction—judgment of the wrongness of you.

In this chapter, I'd like to talk about a particularly insidious and destructive form of judgment that people with addictions engage in. I call it the wrongness of you. It is some form of compulsively and continuously judging yourself as wrong, bad or less-than. Even culturally approved addictions like workaholism or perfectionism have a basis in being inherently wrong. No matter what occurs or what anyone else says or does, you automatically go to the place of how wrong you are. It's a default position, a stance you habitually take that precludes any other alternative.

This pattern gets created very early on. It's the result of young children being told, over and over again, verbally or energetically, that they don't really matter. They are somehow wrong or bad, they don't fit in, they can't get it right or they need to change. Many parents decide it's a kindness to the children to mold them into someone who will fit into what's considered normal. Unfortunately, being "normal" usually comes at the cost of repressing or denying everything that is different and unique about them.

I want to give you what may seem like a silly example of what engaging in the wrongness of you looks like, but please get the energy of it. Imagine a young cardinal, or a redbird, as we call them in Texas. This cardinal has been told from the beginning of its life, "You're a cardinal, and if you want to be a good cardinal, you have to do what the other cardinals in our family do. You have to sit on this branch. You have to sing in this voice. And we want you to make sure you have the right number of feathers." All of a sudden, this beautiful baby cardinal—instead of being the cardinal it is, tries to be the cardinal it is *supposed* to be. It sits on its branch, looks around at the other cardinals, and says, "That cardinal has 497 feathers and I only have 362. What's wrong with me? How do I grow more feathers? That cardinal is singing in a voice that's different from mine. Obviously, my voice is no good. I need to copy that cardinal's voice. I don't think I'm flapping my wings right, and not only that, I'm in the wrong tree. All the other cardinals are in the fir tree and I'm here in this oak tree. Oh, what else have I gotten wrong? What's it going to take for me to fit in and be the cardinal I've been told I have to be?"

Can you imagine a bird heaping that kind of judgment upon itself? The weight of its wrongness would be so great, that it would probably fall out of the tree and die! Or it might start looking for a place it could escape to, so it didn't have to feel the pain of being so utterly wrong.

Isn't it wonderful the birds don't judge themselves? Each one shows up on the tree it chooses with the number of feathers it has and sings in its own voice, in its own individual magnificence, without succumbing to judgment. They have the joyful exuberance that comes from being what they truly are. That's possible for you as well. However, there are so many forces that are geared toward making us fit into the mold that it's not easy for us to come out of the sense that we're wrong.

Another element that serves to teach us that we're wrong comes from our innate egocentricity. Kids are born believing they are the center of the universe—and that's a good thing. If they didn't have that belief, they'd say, "Mom is depressed and Dad is angry. I guess I just won't ask for anything for the next two days." That wouldn't work. Kids have to be egocentric because they don't have the capacity to fulfill their own needs the way adults do. And part of being egocentric is the assumption that everything that happens in their universe is about them and they caused it. So, kids conclude that if someone is angry, it's their fault. If Mom and Dad are fighting, they're to blame. If Mom is sad, they must have been bad.

A client of mine told me that from the time she was a tiny child, she had the feeling that she had come into this life in order to change things for her family and make a difference for them. By the time she was four years old, she realized she wasn't going to be able to do that. No one in her family was about to change anything—and to her, as the small, egocentric being she was, that meant she had failed. It was her fault that the people around her were unhappy and no one was going to change. She clearly recalled a day when was she sitting in the car with her mother, her father and her older sister, and she thought to herself, "Wow, did I ever make a mistake coming in. I thought I could make a difference. How could I have been so wrong?"

The Primary Addiction

My guess is that if you have any sort of addiction, you engage in the wrongness of you. I've never found anyone who had any kind of addictive or compulsive behavior who didn't first have an addiction to the wrongness of them. It shows up differently for different people—but no matter how it shows up, it is always based in judgment of oneself. Without being fully aware of it, you keep going into the wrongness of you. You compulsively and continuously judge how bad and wrong you are.

The addiction to the wrongness of you is actually your primary addiction. And it leads to your secondary addiction—the drinking, the smoking, the drug use, the gambling and so on. The secondary addiction is the place people go to seek relief from the primary addiction to being so very wrong. And until the primary addiction is cleared, it's almost impossible to clear the secondary addiction with any amount of success.

I've seen a great deal of what is called relapse, which occurs when people have stopped engaging in their secondary addictions, and then later go back to them. They stop drinking, overspending or working eighty hours a week. Then, after a period of time, they start doing those things again. This often occurs because when the secondary addiction is taken away, the pain of the primary addiction becomes too difficult for them to manage. They don't have the tools and information they need to move beyond it so they return to their secondary addiction in search of relief. Clearing the primary addiction to the wrongness of you paves the way for you to walk away from your secondary addiction, whatever it may be.

A teenage boy was sent to me because he was addicted to marijuana and acting out in school. He made it clear in the first session that he was not interested in discussing his marijuana use, so we talked about other things that were going on in his life. His parents had been divorced for a couple of years, and he was being criticized in both of their households for his grades, his pot smoking, his failure to do his chores at home and so on. His parents had made him the identified patient, the one who had the problem, but it quickly became clear that both the mother and the father had major issues and behaviors of their own that they were unwilling to look at. As the young man and I worked together, I asked him questions and encouraged him to look at different situations in his life from different perspectives. Was he actually wrong? Was he doing anything that was harmful to his family? What was really going on? How else could he look at this? What did he know to be true?

After a while, he began to have more confidence in himself and he became much happier. He started playing in his band again and stopped judging himself for not fitting in with the more popular kids in school.

We didn't address the marijuana at all during this time. However, after about six months, he came in one day and said, "I want to tell you something that happened yesterday. I was driving home with my friend from school. It's a long drive—about an hour—and that's when we always smoke pot. My friend said, 'Are you ready to light up?' I said, 'You know what? I think I'm going to skip it today.'"

My friend said, "Wow! That's cool."

Besides the success in my client's overcoming the wrongness of him, I'd like to point out how this story illustrates that recovering from addiction is not about focusing on it but rather it's about moving away from all the lies and the sense of wrongness you've had about yourself to a place of the true power and potency of you.

Receiving Judgment

As you move out of wrongness of you and into the space and freedom to be more of you, you're going to have even more judgment directed at you. Any time we change, it makes people uncomfortable. So, what can you do when people throw judgments at you? First of all, remember that a judgment is never about you. It's always about the person who is doing the judging—and it's always arbitrary. Any time you find yourself being judged, just say to yourself, "This is about them and their stuff. It has nothing to do with me."

Here's another tip: People accuse you of what they themselves are doing. If someone accuses you of being unkind, you can bet that *he* or *she* is unkind. If people accuse you of being selfish or cheap, you can bet that that's exactly what *they* are.

Blame, Shame, Guilt and Regret

If you engage in the wrongness of you, blame, shame, guilt and regret are probably a part of what you experience in making yourself wrong. I've met many wonderful people who don't believe they can be a contribution to the world because all of their energy is focused on some real or imagined terrible thing they did in the past.

Blame, shame, guilt and regret always stem from judgments about what's right and wrong. In Access Consciousness®, we call them distracter implants.* They are concepts that have been implanted in us by our parents, the culture and religious organizations in order to control us. Blame, shame, guilt and regret tie us into society and keep us from being aware and knowing what we know to be true for us.

Here's an example of what I mean: When I was six or seven years old, I was in a store, and I thought, "Oh! I could just put some of this candy and gum in my pocket and leave." So, I did that. Later I felt terrible about it. It wasn't shame or guilt I was feeling; I simply knew that behavior wasn't correct for me. My knowing was very simple and straightforward. It was, "I'm not the kind of person who does this." If shame and guilt had been piled upon me, they would have distracted me from knowing what I knew. I would have been immobilized by the feeling, "I'm a bad, terrible, horrible person."

Distracter implants distract us from our knowing and awareness and put us into judgment of how wrong we are. And as long as we are in judgment of how wrong we are, we cannot be aware. When you do something that isn't compatible with who you are, you don't need to experience a bunch of blame, shame, guilt and regret to keep you from doing it again. You can simply say, "That didn't work for me. I don't think I'm going to do that again."

Let's say you got angry and you yelled at your dog. There's a big difference between going into, "Oh, I feel so guilty about yelling at my dog," and

---

*Blame, shame, guilt and regret are just a few of the distracter implants discussed in Access Consciousness, and many of them relate to addiction. More information about all of the distracter implants is available in the Access Foundation and Level One classes.

saying, "Yelling at the dog was not kind to me—or the dog. That was not my best choice. What choice could I make now? Do I need to set things right in some way?"

I'm not saying you shouldn't be aware when you choose to do things that go against the person you truly are. Of course you should be aware of how what you do affects you and the other beings in your life. What I'm talking about is not going into the judgment of wrongness. Guilt eats away at you and distracts you from what's generative in your life. And people use it to control you. "Do you remember that bad thing you did to me ten years ago? I never got over that." What a bunch of hooey! Everybody is responsible for moving on. That's one of the ways guilt is used to control people.

Another way guilt is used to control people is to make everything that's fun and interesting a sin. "You shouldn't enjoy sex. You shouldn't enjoy wonderful food. You shouldn't enjoy having money. You should work full time and more. What are you doing out there, lolling around in the afternoon, enjoying the sun on your face?" Guilt is a great way to encourage people to beat up on themselves and to make sure they don't have a joyful, happy experience in life.

When you find yourself in blame, shame, guilt or regret, recognize that this is not who you are. They are distracters that were implanted into you in order to control you. Without them, you become uncontrollable, not out of control—but uncontrollable. You have more of an opportunity to be the master of your own life and to choose who you would like to be.

If you encounter a sense of blame, shame, guilt or regret that you can't seem to get beyond, ask:

- Who does this belong to?

If that doesn't lighten it up, ask:

- Is this a distracter implant?

If that lightens it up, all you have to do is use the clearing statement to clear everything holding the distracter implant in place.

You can also do the Expanding Out Exercise. When you expand out, you allow the judgment to pass through you. The more expanded out you are and the more you are the space of you, the less you will be the effect of other people's judgments.

It's worth noting that people judge you in order to control you. Judgment is a way of making a wildly wonderful and innately unique individual fit in and become compliant to the values and customs of the group. But here's the thing: You don't fit in. You never have and you never will, and that's actually a plus. You are different from anyone else, and when you recognize this and you don't attempt to fit in, you have the possibility of becoming the amazing being you truly are.

If someone throws a judgment at you that matches one you have of yourself, you'll tend to think the judgment is correct. As soon as you buy someone's judgment as real, you belong to them. Someone may say something like, "You're not trying hard enough." If you've already decided you're a sluffer, you'll immediately go into the wrongness of you and think they're correct. They're not correct; it's that their judgment matched one you already had of yourself. When you become aware you have that judgment, you have the opportunity to let it go.

Buying into other people's judgments of you is always a choice. Are you willing to choose not to validate anyone else's judgments?

Are You Judging Someone Else?

Here's another interesting thing about judgment. Sometimes you might think you're judging somebody else—but it's not you who is doing the judging. That person is judging himself or herself, and you're picking up on the judgment and thinking it's yours.

Once I was walking behind a woman who was very heavy, and I found myself thinking, "That's a lot of fat."

I said, "Wait a minute! I don't really have a point of view about bodies," and I realized I was picking up her judgment of herself.

If you have decided that you are a judgmental person, you're probably not. People who are judgmental never think they are. They always think they're just telling the truth. They'll say, "I'm not a judgmental person. I just know what's true." Actually, they *are* judgmental—but they're not willing to see it.

Letting Go of Judgment

Why are so many of us resistant to letting go of judgment? It may be because we have bought so many of the lies about what judgment does. I often hear people say things like, "If I don't judge myself, I won't be motivated to do anything."

I'd like to ask you a question: What if you didn't motivate yourself from judgment? What if you motivated yourself from choice? What would that be like? Being motivated from judgment puts you in the place of wrongness, where you're always striving to do better. Being motivated from choice takes all the wrongness away. You do whatever you do because you choose to do it. It's not about getting it right or wrong.

I've also heard, "If I let go of judgment, I'll do bad and terrible things."

I always ask, "Who does that belong to?" And then I ask, "Is that statement actually true? Does that statement actually acknowledge the truth of who you are?" This is a great time to use the heavy/light tool.

People also say, "If I let go of judgment, I will be so different from everyone else. I will be alone." Well, that's something that people do find to be true. When you let go of judgment, you're going to be very different. A lot of people use judgment as the main way they connect with others. You can see this in the way fans band

Developing Your Talents and Abilities

One of the things I hear from my clients when we talk about becoming more of who they are is, "Marilyn, I don't really believe that what you say is possible for me, not because people can't change but because I don't think I have anything to offer. My whole life I've tried to contribute things to people or show them my ideas and I always get shut down. I get told I'm stupid or not good enough or even worse, I get ignored. I have a sense that even if I clear my addiction, there's not going to be anywhere for me to go that isn't sad and depressing."

There are many reasons why we end up judging ourselves as having nothing to offer the world, and then we carry that forward as if it were the truth. It's not the truth! Please know that you do have gifts. You do have talents and abilities. And by using the tools in this book and letting go of your limiting belief systems and what others have told you about you, life can expand for you. You will be able to show up in ways you never imagined.

Instead of going to the wrongness of you, begin to have fun with the idea of developing your talents and abilities. Start by asking questions like:

- What would I like to do?
- What would I like to learn?
- What would be fun for me to do?
- What have I always been interested in?
- What energizes me?
- What have I thought I'd like to do but have never tried?

Go toward any activity that seems light for you.

Please have fun with this and start exploring. Discover what you like to do, see what brings you pleasure and you'll begin to get a sense of what your talents and abilities are.

together to root for a sports team, the way the public take sides for and against candidates in an election, or in the way people form in-groups and out-groups.

Please know, however, that there are people all over the world who are beginning to let go of judgment. If you're willing to do that as well, and if you're willing to show up as you, people will begin to appear in your life who are vibrationally compatible with you, the new you, the real you.

Right now, though, you may not have many people like that in your life because if you're judging, you're going to be energetically compatible with other people who are judging. It may look like there's no one in the world who's not judging, but as you begin to show up with a different energy, people who have an energy similar to yours will begin to appear in your life.

Please look at the reasons you may have decided you can't let go of judgment, because those decisions are stopping you from ending addiction and letting go of other limiting behaviors.

Some Things You Can Do to Let Go of Judgment

Once you become aware of the ways you're making judgment right, good, necessary and correct, there are tools you can use and activities you can engage in that will help you to let go of the judgments that keep you from being all of you.

As you read through these suggestions, I encourage you to choose the tools, exercises and activities that resonate with you. Try them out and see whether they help you to feel more expanded and free of judgment. This is all about honoring you and what you know to be true for you.

Tool: Interesting Point of View*

What if everything in your life was just an interesting point of view? The tool, "Interesting Point of View", is a great way to neutralize judgment by reminding yourself that whatever the judgment is, it's just a point of view. It's not right or wrong or good or bad. It's just a belief, opinion, conclusion or some other form of judgment that you or someone else has at this moment in time.

Any time a judgment comes up for you, just say, "Interesting point of view, I have this judgment." It helps to distance you from the judgment. You don't align and agree with it—and you don't resist and react to it. You just allow it to be what it is—a point of view.

Or say someone tells you that you're wrong for this or that reason. You can say, "Wow, that's an interesting point of view. Never mind, I don't think I'll buy it."

When you're functioning from interesting point of view, you're able to be aware of what is, rather than becoming the effect of judgments, whether they're yours or other people's. This matters—because your point of view creates your reality. If you're not in interesting point of view, you get mired in judgment. You cut off your awareness and solidify any difficulties that are present rather than allowing for different possibilities to come through.

I recently flew into the U.S. from Costa Rica. The line to Immigration was very long, and I had a rather tight connection. I began to worry I was going to miss my plane. I started saying, "Interesting point of view that I have the judgment I'm going to miss my plane. What else is possible?" I kept saying that and asking questions, and all of a sudden, another eight immigration agents were moved into our section, and I was the second person in line. I made my connection with no problem.

---

*"Interesting Point of View" is an Access Consciousness® tool.

This might seem like a coincidence, but things like this happen all the time when I use the tool, "Interesting point of view." Letting go of my investment in what the situation appears to be creates a space where other possibilities can show up.

Tool: Who Does This Belong To?*

I've already talked about the tool, "Who does this belong to?" but I want to mention it again in this chapter because it can be a key tool in working with your primary addiction, the addiction to the wrongness of you. Whenever you have a thought, feeling or emotion that has to do with how wrong, bad or less-than you are, don't automatically buy it as yours. Ask, "Who does this belong to?" If it lightens up at all, it's not yours. Just return it to sender.

"Who does this belong to?" is also incredibly helpful in dealing with your secondary addiction. One of my secondary addictions was to alcohol. Now I can have a glass of wine or not; it doesn't matter. I don't have the compulsion to have a drink any more. One day not long ago, I was driving home from work. I'd had a very nice day, and it was about 5:00. It was that time. All of a sudden I had the thought, "I really need a drink. A stiff scotch would be great."

I said, "Wait a minute! I don't even drink scotch. Who does this belong to?" I realized I was picking up the idea that I needed a drink from all the people who were driving home and thinking, "It's 5 o'clock. I need a drink."

Give Yourself a Judgment-Free Day—or a Judgment-Free Hour

What would it be like to have a whole day, or even an hour, where you refused to judge yourself or anything else? This can be a great habit to cultivate. Just say to yourself, "I'm giving myself a judgment-free hour from nine to ten." Then every time a judgment

---

*"Who Does This Belong To?" is an Access Consciousness® tool.

comes up, say, "Sorry, this is my judgment-free time. I'm not having any judgments until ten. Come back after that." As you get more practiced in being judgment free, keep expanding that time period.

Spend Time with People Who Are Less Judgmental

Take a few moments to make a list of the main people in your life. Then rate them, on a scale of one to ten, as to how much they judge you or others. Make it a point to spend time with people who are less judgmental and notice how different the energy is.

Practice Being Present

Find a time when you can take a walk outside in nature, and as you're walking, allow yourself to be aware of everything around you: the way your feet feel on the ground, the sounds, the smells and what's going on with your body. Be as present as you possibly can. Now notice: Can you judge when you're doing this? No. You can't be present and judge at the same time.

Another wonderful thing about being in nature is that nature never judges. So, as you're taking a walk, you can also become aware of the energy of an environment with no judgment.

CHAPTER SIX

Abuse and Addiction

That which you are unwilling to be aware of owns you.

I f you have an addiction, I can just about guarantee that you've experienced some form of abusive behavior earlier in your life. I'm not saying this as an invitation to blame someone or rationalize why your life hasn't worked out the way you wished. I'm bringing it up because it's helpful information. Once you understand the link between addiction and abuse and how it has played out in your life, you will be much more able to move beyond your addictive or compulsive behavior.

Many of my clients with addictions have told me, "I don't understand why I keep acting out with my addictive behavior. I keep overeating, I keep working compulsively or I keep making everyone wrong, even though I want to stop. No matter how hard I try, I keep doing it. It seems unconscious."

This is often the case in the way we act out with our addictions, and it can occur because we have experiences of abuse we don't want to be aware of. I understand that you may not wish to look at something that seems as difficult to deal with as abuse, and you may be asking, "Why do I have to do that?" The answer is quite concise: Because that which you are unwilling to be aware of owns you. If you're unwilling to be aware of the abuse you experienced, if you're trying to exclude it or rationalize it, it will actually run your life. The willingness to become aware of past abuse creates a space where you can change how it affects you now.

I want to make something very clear here. Please know I am not talking about dredging up every incident of abuse in your past and making it the cause of your addiction. Nor am I saying you should spend weeks, months or years mucking around in it. Looking at what was abusive about your past is not about blaming other people or becoming a victim. It's about not pretending you are powerless. It's about acknowledging what happened to you and how it has affected you—so that the abuse doesn't continue to own you.

The Link Between Abuse and Addiction

When we suffer abuse, we want to escape. We want to escape the abuse itself—and later we want to escape the memories of the abuse. The pain of this can seem so great and the prospect of dealing with it so overwhelming that turning to addiction seems like a natural thing to do. The addiction appears to offer a safe haven we can retreat to. This is especially true when we don't have the support we need to move beyond the abuse.

Abuse and addiction are perfect complements to one another because they both lead people to create a smaller life. Almost everyone I've known who has suffered abuse, particularly chronic and ongoing abuse, has created a tiny, hidden life. Why would they do that? Because they made a decision that a small life is safer. They move into a contracted place where they become hyper-vigilant and try to control everything that happens. The thing is, trying to control what happens only gives them the illusion of safety—and it creates so much stress that before long, they begin to yearn for a space where they can be out of control—which is something else that addiction offers.

Identifying Abuse for What It Is

So, what is abuse? Many people don't recognize they were abused because they think that the term *abuse* only refers to sexual abuse or to extreme physical maltreatment. When asked if they were abused, they'll reply, "No, I wasn't abused. I wasn't raped or beaten."

Abuse encompasses much more than physical violence or sexual violation, and there are many forms of abuse that are not always recognized as such. So, how do you identify it? The core of abuse is always about diminishing, degrading or devaluing the being or the body. It's the opposite of honoring you or treating you and your body with respect and regard. If you remember this core characteristic of abuse, you can always see it for what it is.

Abuse can be done by parents, siblings, other kids, teachers and family members. It can also show up in institutions through the dogma or rules and regulations of churches, fraternities, the military and other organizations. Some people abuse others simply because they can. They're inherently mean and don't care about the effect their behavior has on the other person or they are actively seeking to do harm. Abuse can also be done by individuals who think that others need to be reined in, disciplined and controlled for their own good. They've told themselves—and they may even honestly believe—the abusive behavior is for the other person's development. They don't mean to inflict harm, and they rarely see the damage they do.

There is an aspect of abuse that is important to be aware of. Kids who have been abused become so accustomed to being mistreated, punished and pushed around that they don't recognize abuse for what it is. It seems "normal" to them. If you don't recognize abuse for what it is, you can't see the effects it has had on you—and you're apt to abuse others in the same way. If you're not aware of the abusive nature of the behavior, it's simply part of what you learn and you may inflict it on other people.

Sometimes clients come to me who are in terrible conflict about their cruel behavior toward others. They recognize that they're being abusive and they want to do something about it—but they don't know how to change. They have picked up abusive behavior patterns from their family and they don't have the skills to choose something different. The difference between these people and those who willfully abuse others is that the former are aware that their behavior is not consistent with who they want to be and that it harms other people. And they're looking to change it.

There's one other point I'd like to make: There's no excuse for abuse. Regardless of the type of abuse you may have experienced, it's important to see it for what it was—and not to minimize or justify it. Sometimes people who have been abused attempt to understand or rationalize the abuse they received by saying things like, "My abuser was abusive to me because he or she was abused as a child." This may be true in a limited number of circumstances, but generally that argument doesn't hold any water. If being abused would cause someone to abuse others, then every single person who was abused would now be abusing others—and we know that's not happening.

You Can Get Past Abuse

This may be a difficult chapter for you. It may bring up things you do not wish to look at. What I want to say up front is that you can get past your abuse. It will require work, and you may experience some discomfort. Things may even seem very intense or difficult for a while, but I want to assure you that you can get past it—and it's all in the service of no longer being captive to addictive or compulsive behavior.

Forms Abuse Can Take

There are many forms abuse can take, and I would like to talk about some of the more common ways it shows up:

Verbal Abuse   Physical Abuse

Self Abuse   Psychological or Emotional Abuse

Neglect   Financial Abuse

Violations of Privacy   Sexual Abuse

Spiritual Abuse

Verbal Abuse

Verbal abuse is just what it says; it's abuse that is spoken. It's name-calling, criticism and put-down. It's anything that's said to make you feel less-than, unworthy, wrong or incompetent. It can be very subtle, as often people try to cover over the abuse with justifications. For example, parents sometimes explain away their verbally abusive behavior with statements like, "I'm only telling you what you're doing wrong so you can improve yourself."

Well, there are other ways of helping children (or anyone) see that they might make different choices. Does continuous criticism expand and assist people or does it diminish them? Instead of saying, "That's a stupid way to do that" or "You never get things right," or "I just noticed you're doing that wrong," one could ask the person, "Is doing that getting the results you would like? No? I wonder if there is a different approach you could take."

Sometimes parents try to mask their verbal abuse by telling a child, "I'm being tough on you because I love you." Please know that someone who truly cares about you is not going to be highly critical and abusive of you. People also try to characterize their verbal abuse as a joke. If you react to their nasty or demeaning comment, they ask, "Can't you take a joke?" If anybody tries the joke thing with you, remember that jokes are meant to amuse you. They're supposed to make you relax and laugh. If you find yourself contracting and feeling worse, it was not a joke and it was never meant to be one. It was verbal abuse.

Another form of verbal abuse is teasing. People who tease operate from the pretense that they're caring, but if you've been teased as a child, you know how hurtful it can feel and how inherently mean it actually is.

Psychological or Emotional Abuse

Psychological or emotional abuse is verbal abuse on steroids. There is a greater intent to tear the person down, to humiliate, ridicule or keep him or her in a state of terror and fear. Psychological and emotional abuse occurs in the workplace or in school when managers or teachers call people out in public or hold them up to ridicule. It takes place in churches or spiritual groups when religious leaders single someone out as a sinner. The idea is to make someone a scapegoat or an example for others.

An extreme example of psychological or emotional abuse is found in the way concentration camp prisoners are systematically broken down. Less intense yet still destructive forms of emotional abuse commonly show up in families with comments or accusations like, "I know you're lying. You always lie," or "What did you do last night? I know you did something wrong." It's the sense that the abuser holds you in perpetual wrongness, which contributes to the sense of a wrongness you have for yourself.

It's common for people to be emotionally abusive to individuals who engage in addictive behavior. "Why do you have to eat that piece of chocolate cake? You're already fat." "You just had to have that cigarette, didn't you? Now your breath stinks. Can't you be more considerate of me?" These kinds of comments are abusive because their intent is to diminish and demean people.

Taunting and bullying are forms of psychological and emotional abuse as well. These forms of abuse can also involve exerting severe control over another person. I once worked with a family where the husband kept the car keys and the only way the wife could ever have the car was if she asked him for the keys, told him exactly where she was going, when she would be back, and who she was going to be with. She also had to check in with him every hour, on the hour.

Psychological and emotional abuse is also about undermining a person's talents. I had a client who, as a child, was a budding actress, singer and performer. Her father would purposefully make her late to performances, all the while joking about it, "Ha-ha, you're going to be late. You're going to forget your lines." This was an overtly cruel form of psychological abuse.

Sometimes the abuse is not quite as direct as the examples given above. Psychological or emotional abuse often shows up in cases of divorce, where one parent constantly diminishes and devalues the other parent in front of the children. It can also take the form of a parent encouraging a child to act as the parent's significant other. When a parent uses a young child as a sounding board for their emotional or romantic problems or exposes the child to discussions that aren't appropriate for children, it's a form of psychological or emotional abuse. I had a client whose divorced father began using her as a sounding board for his emotional and romantic problems when she was only seven years old. A child should be allowed to be a child—and not be turned into a partner, therapist, caretaker or a confidante for a parent.

Violations of Privacy

Violations of privacy are a variation of emotional abuse. When someone reads your emails or diaries or searches your room, it is emotionally abusive because it gives you the message that you can't have anything that's yours. Everything you are is open to inspection by somebody who has decided you need to be watched or monitored. It's difficult to have a sense of the greatness of you when you are being intruded on in this way. Parents often do this to children, and sometimes husbands and wives do it to one another. It always indicates that the person is not honoring the other as the individual he or she is.

Violations of privacy sometimes cross the line into sexual abuse when an adult doesn't respect a child's right to the privacy of his or her body.

There is a caveat here. If a parent determines that a child is suicidal, heavily into drugs or planning something dangerous, it's appropriate to intervene. There are no hard and fast rules about this; you have to look at the energy of the situation. Is the action being taken to truly assist the child—or does it stem from the parent's need to dominate and control?

Physical Abuse

Physical abuse is any kind of pushing, shoving, slapping or hitting. It includes being physically beaten up, struck with objects, tied up or burned. It's anything that people do to inflict pain upon the body of another.

When I ask clients if they have been physically abused, many of them say things like, "Oh no, I mean my mom beat me with a belt occasionally, but it wasn't that bad. And once my Dad pushed me down the stairs, but I deserved it." The notion that you deserve to be abused is a lie. In fact, it's one of the biggest lies perpetrated upon kids who are abused. "My father shoved me into the cabinets because I upset him. He didn't mean to break my arm." "Well, yeah, my dad did punch me in the face and break my nose, but I was talking back." None of that is acceptable behavior. You did not deserve it. And you don't need to minimize, justify or explain it. You don't deserve physical abuse—ever.

Neglect

Neglect can be physical or emotional. As children, we need food, shelter, clothing and other physical necessities. We also have basic emotional needs that include eye contact, acknowledgment, touch, attention and a sense that we matter. When we don't get these things, we are being neglected.

Sometimes I see clients who seem to have many of the characteristics associated with having been abused, but when I ask if there has been any abuse in their lives, they say no. When I probe a little further, I find that they were neglected. They had food and shelter, but they were not held, nurtured and made to feel cared for. Or they were latchkey kids from the time they were three or four years old and basically had to fend for themselves.

Neglect is a subtle form of abuse because it's not about what was done to you; it's about what *wasn't* done. If you did not have your basic physical and emotional needs met, you may have a sense that somehow you're wrong, undesirable or not deserving. Just because someone didn't give you what you required, doesn't mean you didn't deserve it, require it or have a right to it. Neglect, like physical or emotional abuse, is a significant form of abuse, and its effects can be equally long lasting.

Sexual Abuse

Sexual abuse occurs when one person forces undesired sexual behavior on another. When children are involved, it is any behavior by an adult (or older adolescent) whose purpose is to sexually stimulate either themselves or the child. This includes inappropriate touching, sexual contact, exposing one's body to a child with intent to gratify one's own sexual desires or asking or pressuring a child to engage in sexual activities. It can also involve displaying pornography to a child or using a child to produce pornography.

Many people who have been sexually abused have difficulty with relationships of any kind because of that intimate violation. They may not have a healthy relationship with their own body—or with the people in their life. And a legacy of sexual abuse often makes people particularly prone to addictive or compulsive behavior. If this is true for you, please know that this is not due to an inherent wrongness in you—and that you can get past it. Restoring your relationship with yourself and your body and stepping into who you truly are, is a great antidote to the effects of abuse.

Looking at any form of abuse is about seeing what is and knowing what you know. There are no one-size-fits-all conclusions we can make about it. Being present with the abuse you may have experienced is about being in your awareness of people and situations. I would like to tell you about an extraordinary man who was able to get past the abuse he experienced because he was willing to be in his awareness and ask questions.

This man told me that he had been severely sexually and physically abused as a child. He had done a lot of work on the abuse with Gary Douglas, the founder of Access Consciousness®, and he couldn't figure out why he wasn't getting past it. Gary was approaching this man's abuse from the conclusion that abuse was a terrible thing that should never happen to a child. But as they continued to work together, the man said he was feeling more and more like he was encased in cement. Why wasn't it getting lighter? Then one day Gary said to him, "This is a crazy question, but did you have some part in creating the abuse you experienced?"

All of a sudden, the man's universe lightened up, and he said, "Yes, I did. I don't know exactly what part I played in creating it, but yes, I played a part in it. What could that be?"

As Gary and the man worked together, the man realized that he, as a six-year-old child, had put himself in the way of the abuse to prevent others from having to receive it. He knew that if he didn't do that, the abuser was going to assault a lot of other children. He actually made the choice to be abused—and the result was that he was able to act in such a way that the abuser was found out. In the end, the abuser actually got some help and was able to turn his life around.

You may wish to ask yourself the same question that Gary asked the man. "Did I have some part in creating the abuse I experienced?" Was I willing to take on the abuse because I was protecting someone else from having it?" Maybe you were protecting your siblings. Maybe you had the knowing that if that person abused you, he or she would be found out—and that would prevent others from being molested or harmed. Do you have any idea how intrinsically kind and caring you can be in your willingness to sacrifice yourself for others?

Use the heavy/light tool as you ask yourself this question:

- Did I have some part in creating the abuse I experienced?

Clearly, this will not be true for everyone, but if it's light, there is some truth in it for you. It's about being aware and uncovering any lies you've been telling yourself. I want to put this possibility out there for you to consider, because if it's true for you and you don't acknowledge it, you're not going to see what is. You'll be operating out of a fantasy or from somebody else's point of view, and that's not going to set you free.

If you choose to work with a counselor who can assist you with issues relating to sexual abuse, I encourage you to find someone who does not have fixed ideas about abuse. Working with a judgment-free person will allow you to see what actually happened because, as this story demonstrates, sometimes we choose to create abuse in order to stop the abuser from mistreating others. If that's true of you, and you're working with a counselor whose attitude is, "That was terrible, that was awful, that should never have happened to you," it will create a kink in your universe. You won't be able to see the experience for what it actually was—and you won't be able to fully release it.

It's also important to point out that not every person who experiences abuse reacts in the same way. There are many different factors that determine how people respond to abuse, including their temperament, whether they told an adult at the time, whether they were believed and acknowledged, and the duration and severity of the abuse.

There are some other aspects of sexual abuse that it's helpful to be aware of. For example, being touched and stroked feels good to the body, and many children walk away from sexual abuse with shame and guilt. They know it was wrong, they know the abuse should not have happened, and they say, "But I enjoyed it." Of course part of them enjoyed it, because bodies love touch. It's stimulating—and children are very sensuous. Have you ever watched a baby? I once went to a party and there was a two-month-old baby in his mother's arms, being breastfed. One of his hands was on his mother's breast, and the other one was holding his little penis. He was so happy because of the wonderful sensations in his body. The joy of that little baby! Our bodies love sensation. So, if you were sexually abused and you enjoyed any part of it, please don't judge yourself for that.

Another aspect of sexual abuse that can be confusing relates to our ability to perceive other people's feelings, thoughts and emotions. Perpetrators of sexual abuse are aware that what they're doing is wrong, and they often carry a sense of shame or judgment, not to mention other complicated emotions. Children often misidentify those feelings as their own. They aren't able to get free of these until they acknowledge that those feelings, thoughts and emotions weren't theirs to begin with.

Self Abuse

Generally we think of abuse as something one person does to another, but one of the forms of abuse is self abuse or self injury. You cut yourself, starve yourself, deprive yourself, enforce very rigid, high standards on yourself or punish yourself in some way. Addiction is a classic example of self abuse. Self judgment is also a form of self abuse, because the core of abuse is always about diminishing or devaluing the body or the being—and that's exactly what self judgment does. It can be saying mean things to yourself like, "I hate myself," "I'm stupid," "My body is ugly and fat," "I look so old," or anything else that diminishes you and/or your body. While you may have moved past other forms of abuse, this one may still be very active for you. I encourage you to be aware of how you treat yourself. Self abuse can be one of the most destructive forms of abuse there is, and it tends to lock people into their addictive or compulsive behavior.

Financial Abuse

Financial Abuse is another form of abuse that's often not recognized. I had a client whose parents had adequate funds, yet when she was ten years old, they told her she was responsible for paying her portion of the household expenses and they sent her out to work twelve-hour days picking vegetables with migrant workers. I recognize that there are times when parents don't have enough money, and children are required to work, but this was not one of those circumstances. It was done to diminish the girl and let her know she wasn't worth supporting.

The difference between financial abuse and lack of resources lies in the intention, energy and attitude of the parents. When children know they are loved and cared for, they don't take on the idea that they are undeserving and worthless. But when they are exposed to comments like, "You're costing us too much money," or "You're a real financial burden to us," they can come away with a distorted idea of their worth and basic value.

Financial abuse creates havoc in the way people think about money and it reinforces the idea of scarcity. But more than that, because money is so connected with our idea of the value of things, children who have been financially abused come to the conclusion that they're valueless and that even their most basic needs cost too much.

Spiritual Abuse

If you were told you had to believe in a certain religion or accept certain beliefs or ways of being, it was spiritual abuse. Were you told you were going to hell or that you were wrong in God's eyes? That was abuse—because it was not honoring of you. My point of view is that anyone who is a true friend and a helpful person in your life will encourage you to choose the spiritual or religious path you'd like to pursue. The one that's right for you. You get to choose your belief system. If you want to go to awareness and consciousness, you get to choose that. If you want to go with a traditional religion, you get to choose that. If you choose to have no religion at all, that's fine too.

Nobody has the right to tell you what you should believe in and that you're wrong if you don't share their beliefs.

Some Factors That Influence the Effects of Abuse

Early in my career, I worked in a psychiatric hospital with children who had been abused. Often they had been sexually abused. We found in these cases—and this is also noted in the research—that the children recovered much more quickly if, after the parents found out about the abuse, they immediately filed charges against the perpetrator and helped the child to see that it wasn't his or her fault; the child had not done anything wrong and didn't deserve to be treated that way. When this occurred, kids could move past the abuse, even when it had been extreme. But if no one acknowledged the abuse, if the child told a parent and the parent did nothing, or if a parent was involved in the abuse or told the child that he or she was making it up, then the effects of that abuse became much more severe.

Perhaps you were abused and never told anyone about what you experienced. Or maybe you did tell someone, but you weren't believed. No one said, "You didn't deserve to be treated like that, and I'm going to do everything I can to protect you from now on." Or perhaps you told someone, and that person said, "Get over it. You're too sensitive," or "You're making that up," or "So-and-so would never do the things you're saying," or "You deserved it. It was your fault. You're a bad girl or a bad boy." Those kinds of responses increase and prolong the effects of the abuse and set you up for the diminishment that makes addictive and compulsive behavior a more appealing choice.

Abuse Affects Your Body and Your Being

Your body and your being are intimately connected, so no matter what form abuse takes, both body and being are affected. For example, the after-effects of verbal or psychological abuse are often evident in people's bodies. They tend to walk around looking physically diminished, with their shoulders stooped or hunched over. It may seem like they want to disappear. And people who have suffered physical abuse are often impacted emotionally and psychologically. They may hold themselves back or be reluctant to speak. They may have no self-confidence.

For many of these people, the response to abuse is to decide such things as: "I can't trust other people. I don't have the power to stop abuse. I can't be me without putting up a lot of barriers and building a fortress. I'm not sure I want to be me, anyway, because obviously me isn't worth anything, otherwise, I wouldn't have been treated like this in the first place. People aren't going to be kind to me. Maybe I need to take any relationship, any situation, any job that comes my way because that's all a loser like me deserves. I know this person isn't going to be kind to me, but any attention, even if it's bad attention, is better than no attention at all." Can you see where these decisions and conclusions create a psychological and emotional environment where addiction can seem like a welcoming option?

One of the reasons that abuse gets such a stronghold on us is that it often begins very early on, before we have the concept that life could be anything other than abusive. We think abuse is normal. Here's an interesting fact about abuse: People who were not abused as children rarely grow up to be adults who are abused. Adults who have not experienced abuse as children are much more apt to recognize and reject an abusive person or situation because it does not feel "normal" to them, the way it does to someone who was abused as a child.

I had a client who came in one day and said, "I don't understand it. I keep attracting abusive men into my life."

I responded, "It's not that you attract abusive men. Abusive men are looking for a place to settle. They'll go to Betty, then to Sarah, Mary and Ellen—and Betty, Sarah, Mary and Ellen all say, "No way I'm going to be with you!"

Then the abusive guy goes to you, and you say, "Sure, come on in!" He has found his target. People who are looking for an abusive relationship are seeking someone who will accept an abusive partner.

It's About Getting Clear on What Is

As you reflect on this summary of the more common forms abuse takes, I encourage you to look at any abuse you may have experienced and to ask:

- As the result of this abuse, what decisions, judgments and conclusions have I come to about my life, my future and what was possible for me?

- How has the abuse affected my life, my relationships and my body?

The first step in moving beyond abuse is always about acknowledging the abuse that occurred. It's not about dwelling in the past, it's not about focusing on how you've been a victim, and it's not about explaining why you can't have the life you would like to have. You can always move beyond abuse and its after-effects—but you have to make a conscious choice to do that. In the next chapter, I'll talk about these after-effects and some ways you can begin to move beyond abuse.

CHAPTER SEVEN

Moving Beyond Abuse

*If you recognize some of the signs and symptoms of abuse in yourself,
I hope it will encourage you to ask questions and take a fresh look
at how past abuse may be tied to your addictive or
compulsive behavior.*

Occasionally when I'm working with someone who has an addiction and I ask about abuse, he or she will say, "Oh, yeah, I was abused, but I've already dealt with that."

I reply, "If you've truly dealt with the abuse, you probably would not be having the issues with addiction that you're still having."

When you make a decision like, "That's concluded, that's done," it takes you out of the question, and the thing that will give you the most freedom from abuse—or anything else that limits you—is the willingness to be in the question.

Another point of view that prevents people from moving beyond the abuse they experienced relates to the fact that some abuse is subtle, and when it has been an ongoing part of a person's life, it comes to seem "normal". It's hard to see it for what it is. So, in this chapter, I'd like to approach abuse from a different perspective and talk about the signs and symptoms that indicate abuse has been present in a person's life. If you recognize some of these signs and symptoms in yourself, I hope it will encourage you to ask questions and take a fresh look at how abuse may be tied to your addictive or compulsive behavior.

Recognizing the Signs and Symptoms of Abuse
Surviving Rather Than Thriving

One of the signs of past abuse is surviving rather than thriving. Surviving is about a focus on just getting through the day, the week or the month. There is always an anxiety about life— because the idea of survival is that you might not make it. Surviving is about not knowing whether you're going to be safe in the world. It's not knowing whether you can trust yourself. There's no sense that the universe is supporting you or that life is abundant. You have a fairly barren, contracted existence. If you're surviving, you may not have much joy in your life at all, because joy is considered a luxury.

Thriving is about knowing that you can create the life you desire to have. It's about expansion, joy and the sense that anything is possible. Thriving is not about having enormous numbers of things. It's about knowing that the universe is an abundant and friendly place. Einstein is quoted as saying, "The most important question for people is 'Is the universe friendly?'" Surviving is coming up with the answer no. Thriving is knowing the answer is yes.

So, please look at whether you are thriving—or just surviving.

Seeing Oneself as the Effect of Other People and Circumstances

One of the things I have found, and this ties in with the idea of surviving vs thriving, is that people who have been abused tend to see themselves as the effect of other people and circumstances. This isn't difficult to understand if you're a child who is just going along merrily and suddenly you're beaten, sexually abused or cruelly criticized. This kind of treatment, when it occurs over a period of time, encourages you to see yourself as the effect of the people or things in your life rather than the creator of your experience.

Sometimes when I talk with people who see themselves as the effect of life, it strikes me that they are like a beach ball in the middle of the ocean during a storm, in that they have no sense of being in control of any aspect of their existence. It's as if they are being tossed from one wave to another. They are not aware that they can affect their life or future in any way.

Children do not have the control in their lives that adults have, and many adults who were abused as children may still operate from the position that they have no control. Let me ask you a question: Do you know on some level that you can make choices that are going to change your circumstances and create a future that you would truly like to have? Or are you stuck in the idea that life happens to you?

Sometimes when I ask this question, people say, "Wow, I didn't even realize I was stuck in that idea." That's why I want to bring it to your attention. If you see yourself as the effect of people and situations, it blocks you from creating the future you desire. You're always looking to see what's going to happen, how that's going to affect you, and what limited choices or options are within that restricted frame of reference. A much more positive and productive approach is, "I can be aware. I can be the creator of my life."

When being the effect of other people and circumstances becomes a core way of being in the world, it often leads to addictive or compulsive behavior. You habitually choose to be the effect of a substance or a behavior rather than being present and dealing with the situations and circumstances of your life. Check to see how this is operating in your life and notice when you make yourself the effect of a substance or behavior in order to avoid something. Instead of doing that, you can ask, "How could I change this?" or "What would it take to choose something different in this situation?"

Recently a friend of mine found out that her father had terminal cancer. Most of the family went into the trauma, drama and grief of the situation, but my friend made the choice to not do that. She chose to bring as much joy, ease and happiness as she could to her dad and the family's last days with him. Because of her choice, the family was able to step into a place that revolved around their gratitude for their father. The father was able to receive all the acknowledgments of how much he meant to the family, and no one had to live in a place of, "This is awful and terrible." They all experienced joy and peace in the father's final days.

During the Great Depression of the 1930s in the United States, a lot of people decided, "This is a terrible situation. I'm going to be poor. I'm the effect of these circumstances." But there were a number of people who became fantastically wealthy during the Depression because they refused to be the effect of the depressed economy. These weren't people who started out with wealth; rather, they were individuals who were willing to look for possibilities that hadn't existed before. They came from a place of knowing they could generate and create something beyond what everybody else had chosen to be the effect of. On some level, they asked questions like, "What's possible here?" and "What would it take for me to make money?"

When you're not willing to be the effect of circumstances, you see yourself as the creator or source of your life.

Being a Victim

Seeing oneself as a victim is closely related to being the effect of others. I understand that there are times when it appears that you have been the victim of someone else's behavior or some circumstance in your life, but I encourage you not to buy "victim" as an identity or continue to use your past experience as an excuse for not showing up in your life.

Being a Bull in a China Shop

A bull in a china shop is a person who crashes into everything. These people are heedless of others, and they leave a lot of broken dishes and glassware in their wake. This can occur when someone responds to abuse by deciding, "This world is abusive and I'm going to be as heedless of others as they've been of me." The bull in the china shop is the other side of being a victim. Both of them are so-lidified positions a person chooses to act from. Neither stance offers the freedom of having moved beyond the abuse.

Hyper-Vigilance

When you're hyper-vigilant, you're in a constant state of over-drive physically. It's like the state you would be in if a wild animal were chasing you. It's as if the world is dangerous, and you're on the constant lookout for threats to your survival. Hyper-vigilance is not awareness and it's very hard on your body. The antidote to hyper-vigilance is the willingness to be aware.

PTSD

Another sign or symptom of abuse is what in psychology is called PTSD, post-traumatic stress disorder. In PTSD, energies from trau-matic events get locked in the body and brain. People with PTSD have flashbacks of highly traumatic events they've gone through. They experience the past as if it's recurring in the present, over and over again. They tend to be emotionally cut off from others and carry with them a feeling of always being in danger. And they often turn to addictive or compulsive behavior to find some relief from the pain.

There are many effective ways to deal with post-traumatic stress disorder. One of most valuable actions I've discovered combines two body processes from Access Consciousness® that are done by an Access Consciousness® facilitator, the Bars and Tri-fold Sequencing Systems.*

There is a woman in Australia whose husband had been involved in combat as part of a special operations force in the Australian Navy.

---

*If you are interested in finding out more about these body processes, you can locate an Access Consciousness® facilitator in your area through the Access Consciousness® website given at the end of the book.

He had a lot of post-traumatic stress disorder and would sometimes get triggered by his dreams and begin punching her in the middle of the night. She started running his Bars with Tri-fold Sequencing Systems and he got so much peace and relief that his fellow soldiers started asking him, "What are you doing? You're so different!"

When he told them his wife was running some processes on him, they became very interested, and she ended up doing these processes on each individual in his entire division—and it created enormous change for them.

Being Stuck in the Idea That You're Not Good Enough

Another characteristic of people who've been abused is that they don't see what a gift and contribution they are to the world. Even if other people can see the potential they have or the gift they are, the individual who experiences himself or herself as not good enough cannot receive that information. Is that true of you? If so, please know the idea you're not good enough is simply another arbitrary judgment that reinforces the wrongness of you. It's a belief you are operating from, and it's likely due to the abuse you experienced. Your judgments about yourself are not a truth about you—and they can be changed.

These are some of the signs that indicate abuse has been present in your life. If you recognize any of these signs or symptoms in yourself, it may indicate that you are still experiencing the consequences of abuse in your life.

Some Things You Can Do to Move Beyond Abuse

Make Sure the Abuse Is Not Still Occurring

If you have abuse in your past, it is likely that you are choosing to be with abusive people in the present—because that's what seems normal to you. You may, for example, be receiving ongoing verbal abuse from your partner, co-workers, friends or family members.

One of my clients, a woman I will call Susan, experienced verbal and emotional abuse in her childhood. She was not initially aware that a consequence of the abuse in her adult life was that she had chosen "friends" who were demeaning of her. This didn't mean these people didn't have some good qualities or that Susan didn't have fun with them, but these "friends" always seemed to find a way to make themselves look better than Susan and leave her feeling less-than. When Susan finally became aware that their behavior was abusive, she was able to honor herself by letting go of these so-called friendships. This was distressing to her at first, as she didn't have many other friends, but gradually she began to invite people into her life who didn't judge her. These were true friends, who honored and supported her and celebrated her victories and successes.

Have a look around your life right now:

- Do the people in your life truly support and empower you? Or do they judge you?
- Are they demeaning or diminishing of you in any way?

If you have someone in your life who is abusive, you can make the choice to acknowledge that fact and to maintain your relationship with him or her—but my suggestion is that you consider walking away from whatever that relationship is.

Sometimes people justify their abuse of you by pointing out all their wonderful characteristics or the good things they have done. Please don't get caught in the trap of buying their justification. Abuse is abuse, even if there are some positive aspects to a relationship. You don't have to stay in a relationship where you're looking at the ways the good makes up for the bad. Whether the situation is with a friend, a family member or someone else, I encourage you to get out of the abusive situation as soon as you can.

There is never a reason or justification for allowing someone to abuse you.

Make Kindness Something You Actively Observe

If you realize that you have gravitated toward people who are abusive, please know that you can choose to change that. The first step might be to start noticing how people treat one another. Observe relationships that are very different from the ones you're used to. Notice individuals who are caring. Ask other people, "Who do you know that's kind? What could that look like?" Ask the universe, "I'd like to meet some people who are truly supportive, some real friends. What would that take?" and start looking for that.

You can also see examples of kindness and caring by watching TV and movies or reading books. Make kindness something you actively observe. Then you can make it something you look for. It may feel unfamiliar and even uncomfortable for a while, but you can still make it a target, and you can change the energy that has created the current abuse in your life. And here's the bottom line: You know on some level, even if you've denied it, whether someone is being kind or abusive to you. So, go with what you know.

If the Abuse Is No Longer Occurring, Recognize That It's Over

You're in a different place now. It sounds so logical, but many people don't get it. They act as if the abuse is still going on. They continue to operate from a hyper-vigilant place. Once you allow yourself to know that the abuse is actually over, it's like opening a door to a different future.

Look at Whether You May Be Inviting Abuse

If abuse is continuing in your life, there's something else to look at. This may not be an easy question to ask yourself, but it's vital:

Are you inviting abuse in your life? Just because you've been abused doesn't necessarily mean everyone's out to get you. Sometimes people who have been abused actually create and invite abuse.

Many times people who come from abusive childhoods create, consciously or unconsciously, the same abusive circumstances in their marriages or other relationships. I am not trying to blame the victim here, but it's important to look at whether you're recreating the abuse you once experienced. It's not just about the kind of people we create relationships with. It's also about what we tell them and teach them, energetically and with words, about how they should treat us.

I worked with a client who had recently become divorced. I asked him why he left his wife. He said, "I have never hit anyone in my life. My ex-wife had been in three physically abusive relationships with men before she met me, and she kept energetically and verbally goading me to hit her. It was as if she was out to prove that this is what men do—they abuse women. The day I drew my fist back to hit her, I stopped myself and walked out of the house. That was the end of the marriage."

Ask Questions

Ask a lot of questions about the conclusions and decisions you've come to about abuse. Question the belief systems you've bought from people around you. Ask:

- Are the conclusions, decisions and beliefs I've come to about abuse actually mine—or do they belong to someone else?

In this way, you can see what's true for you. And that's important.

Another question I encourage you to ask is:

- What gift did I get from the abuse I experienced?

This is a bit like the question, "What's right about your addiction?" When you begin to see the positive and negative aspects of something, you open yourself up to more possibilities. Look at what that abuse created that has not been helpful to you. But also be open to what that experience is facilitating for you and others in the world.

- Has your experience of abuse given you the awareness required to create a difference in the world?

- Has it made you a stronger person?

- Have you made a demand of yourself to do something to ensure it doesn't happen to other people?

- Or have you made a demand of yourself to always treat others with honor and respect, which is the way you should have been treated but weren't?

Ask yourself these questions and others that may occur to you. You may find that there was a completely unexpected gift in the abuse you experienced.

Practice Saying No

What many children learn from any form of abuse is that they are not in control of their lives. They're at the effect of others and they don't have the right to say *no*. Is this true of you? Do you still have difficulty saying *no*? Do you believe you don't have the right to say no? You know what? You do. You can say *no* in a variety of ways. It's something you can practice—and get good at.

Make it a habit to say *no* to someone or something every day. It can be a small thing, and it can be polite. In a restaurant, you can say, "No thank you. I don't think I'll have any more coffee." You can respond to an invitation with, "No thank you, I'm not interested in going to that movie." You can say *no* to a request, "No, I won't be able to walk your dog while you're away." Or you can say *no* to yourself, "No, I'm not going to have that extra scoop of ice cream."

Another way of saying *no* is to state, "I'm sorry, that doesn't work for me." This doesn't require you to confront the other person or put them on the defensive. You don't owe anyone an explanation for your responses, and if someone tries to pressure you into explaining yourself, you can just keep saying, "I'm sorry, that doesn't work for me." One of the biggest mistakes we make is to believe we owe people explanations, reasons and justifications for our responses, particularly if we're turning them down. But here's the truth: You don't.

"I'm sorry, that doesn't work for me," may not be powerful enough to stop certain people, and that's when you just have to come out and say, "No, I'm not doing that." But "I'm sorry, that doesn't work for me" is a good place to start. Try it and see what you can do with that.

It may also be helpful to playact or practice saying no in front of a mirror. "No, Mom, I'm not coming home for Christmas this year." "No, I'm not going to have those people over today. It doesn't work for me." If you have a friend who supports you and doesn't judge or criticize, ask him or her to practice or roleplay with you. It's not saying *no* from a place of white-knuckling it, but from the sense that you have a real choice.

The capacity to say *no* is crucial to you showing up as yourself—and it's crucial to moving beyond addiction; it also includes (at least in the beginning, while you're still working on it) saying *no* to circumstances that you know can trigger your addictive or compulsive behavior.

I was working with a client who had issues with overeating and bingeing, and she was doing very well for about three weeks. Then one day she sent me an email stating that she had totally failed and was judging herself terribly because she had gone to a party and binged. When I asked her about the circumstances, she told me that she knew in advance that every element of the party offered a trigger for her to binge: the types of food, the amounts of food and the people who were there. What came out of that was an awareness on her part that in the early stages of working on her issues with food, it wasn't helpful or kind to put herself in situations with food that would trigger her. Don't set yourself up for failure. Your addictive or compulsive behavior has been with you for a long time, so give yourself the time, space and the environment you need to get past it. This may involve saying *no* to circumstances that could trigger you.

Listen to CDs and Recorded Classes About Abuse

A number of CDs and recorded classes about clearing the issues of abuse are for sale in the Access Consciousness® shop.* Many people have received enormous healing and change from these. I encourage you to use the heavy/light tool to see if these are something that might assist you in clearing issues of past abuse.eone who will accept an abusive partner.

Get Some Bodywork

A lot of people who have experienced abuse, particularly physical or sexual abuse, don't like their bodies to be touched. But when you feel ready for it, consider getting some bodywork that feels good to you and your body. It can be very helpful and healing for you, because when we experience abuse, we tend to lock it into our bodies.

I've used the Access Consciousness® body processes, with great success, to help me release pain and the after-effects of abuse. There are other modalities as well. Find one that truly works for you.

---

*The Access Consciousness® website is given in the "Resources" section at the back of the book.

Destroy and Uncreate the Past

Here is another simple but very powerful thing you can do: Use the clearing statement to destroy and uncreate your past. Imagine how freeing it would be to destroy and uncreate all the baggage—the decisions, beliefs and other forms of judgment you have brought forward from your past experiences, including past abuse. If you are willing to let go of your past, you can have a completely different future.

Every morning and/or every evening, you simply say:

Everything I've aligned and agreed with and resisted and reacted to before this moment, everything I've solidified and made real, I now revoke, recant, rescind, reclaim, renounce, denounce, destroy and uncreate it all. Right and wrong, good and bad, POD and POC, all 9, shorts, boys and beyonds™.

Please know that you can't destroy and uncreate anything that is actually true. What you're destroying and uncreating are the lies, untruths, judgments and belief systems you adopted in the past that are limiting you in the present.

Tool: That's Not Me

A tool you can use when you find yourself referencing the past and wish to become more present is to say to yourself, "That's not me." You're not the same person you were when you experienced the abuse. Even if you're talking about the past that was ten or twenty seconds ago, you're not the same person you were then. You've changed energetically and the environment has changed as well. So, anytime you notice that you're referencing the past, just remind yourself, "Oh! That's not me."

Practice Gratitude Every Day

Have you noticed that the energy of gratitude is very expansive, whereas the energy of resentment and blame is very contractive? Practicing gratitude can assist you in creating a future that's very different from your past.

I'm not talking about being grateful for your health or other huge things. I'm talking about finding small, specific things you're grateful for and saying why you're grateful for them. I don't usually recommend asking yourself *why* questions, but in this case, looking at why you're grateful for something gives you an indication of what matters to you. And that's good information for you to have. When you put your attention on things you're grateful for, you take the focus away from the pain and problems, and you create an energy that helps you move forward into a more expansive life.

For example, yesterday I was grateful that I got an email from someone who's willing to translate some of my work into Spanish, because it means I can go to Mexico and share the work I'm doing. I was also grateful that my plants are doing well; I love sitting on the patio with them. You can also be grateful for the progress you're making with your addictive or compulsive behavior. You can be grateful to yourself for not taking that fourth cigarette or for refraining from your usual habit of criticizing your child or yourself.

It generally takes three weeks to create a habit, so I encourage you to actively work at this for at least twenty-one days, until being in gratitude becomes a more natural approach for you.

Practice Random Acts of Kindness and Caring

Another thing that you can do is to practice random acts of kindness and caring, both for yourself and others.

Once again, these don't have to be big things. I'm suggesting that you do small things, like smiling at the clerk in the grocery store, picking up something that somebody has dropped, making eye contact and genuinely greeting somebody, or taking a half an hour a day just for you.

Doing small, kind acts like these bring you into the present—and one of the things that will be most helpful to you in moving beyond abuse and addiction is doing whatever you can do to stay present. There's something about smiling at someone, patting a dog or fixing a lovely, healthy meal for yourself that helps you to be more present. And being more present allows for more joy and the possibility of moving beyond abuse and addiction.

CHAPTER EIGHT

Addiction and Bodies

I've never known anyone who was completely at home with his or her body who engaged in addictive or compulsive behavior.

I once asked a group of sober women in a traditional recovery program how they felt about their bodies. They looked at me like I was nuts. Their response was, "Why would you ask that question? Occasionally my body is useful to me, but ugh, it's something I don't like to think about."

I was in that same recovery program for many years, and I had the same point of view about my body. For a great deal of my life, I didn't pay any attention to it. It was something that ate, drank, smoked and sometimes overdid it. Once in a while it was a source of pleasure. Sometimes it was a source of pain, but for the most part, it was something I didn't think about, or at worst, judged and disparaged.

When I look back on that recovery program, I realize that nothing was ever said about the body—except that it had an allergy to alcohol. In other words, my body was part of the problem. It was one of the reasons I was "an alcoholic."

The notion that the body is a problem or something to be disparaged and disregarded reflects a great deal about our culture's way of thinking about bodies. Whether it's because of Judeo-Christian influences, the emphasis on the importance of the mind or some other factors, bodies tend to be relegated to a very lowly position. They're something we have to put up with while we're on planet Earth. Many spiritual and religious traditions actually make the body inferior. It's regarded as the house for the spirit until the spirit can leave the body, go to a better place or become something greater. In our culture, we also tend to associate bodies with animals, which are seen as lower forms of life.

Have you neglected your body by working too many hours, deciding that your to-do list was more important than sleep, overeating or drinking excessive amounts of alcohol? Have you engaged in activities that were harmful to your body? When you get up in the morning, do you look in the mirror and judge your body unmercifully? Have you kicked your body under the bed as something to be ignored? Have you treated your body that way? I did—until I realized what a gift it was.

Part of the antidote to addiction, to you being you, is to embrace the body and all it has to offer. So, I'd like to talk about our bodies and what they have to do with addiction and recovery.

Addiction Is Hard on Your Body

First of all, on a very practical level, addiction is hard on your body. When you engage in any kind of addictive or compulsive behavior, you are not present with your body. You can't receive the information and awareness it has to offer you. And here's an even more important point about addiction and bodies: If you are disconnected from your body, you will never get past your addictive or compulsive behavior. The most you will be able to do is to manage the symptoms in a lifelong program. Why is that? Because your body is crucial to your life and living. You and your body are not the same, but you're intimately connected. Your body can be your partner or your best friend, but if you disconnect from it, you can't be present in a way that will allow you to move past addictive or compulsive behavior.

Few people have the information and tools they need to connect with their body. You were probably taught to see your body as an object. No one ever told you that your body is conscious. Well, I'd like to tell you right now that your body *is* conscious. It has preferences, desires and points of view. Your body is the one that eats, it's the one that wears clothes, it's the one that requires housing. The more you're connected to your body and the more you listen to it, the more these areas of your life are going to be harmonious.

We are all aware of the communications from our body when we experience them as pain. Pain is actually the body's last resort for communicating with you. As you become more aware of your body, you will notice that it also communicates with you in more subtle ways. As this is more energetic than cognitive, it's a little difficult to describe in words. However, if you are willing to practice being more present with your body, you will find yourself becoming more and more aware of the valuable information it has to convey to you.

At one point, I started to reconnect with my body. I still wasn't quite sure how to listen to it, but I was willing to try. I was in a very nice store, and I found a jean jacket on sale. It was only $20. I thought, "Oh! This is so cute! I want this jacket." I tried on the jacket, and in my head, I heard, "You can buy it, but I won't wear it."

My first impulse was to look around the room to see who said that, but actually, I knew it was a voice in my head and I knew it was coming from my body. That was the first time I received a message from my body. I think it was translated into a thought so I could hear it. I now get the messages in more subtle ways. Anyway, I said, "Okay, I won't buy it. What are we going to do now?"

My idea was to leave the store, but the energy said, "No, don't leave."

I said, "Okay, body, this is weird. Is there something here you'd like?"

My body said, "Yes." This time the communication came to me more like an energy.

I was walking around the store, and I suddenly stopped in front of a pair of pink pajamas. I said, "Are you kidding me? Pink pajamas?" I've never been a girly girl, and I had never worn anything remotely like those pink pajamas. But the energy from my body said, "Yeah!" so I bought them.

I have since discovered that my body likes girly things. It was happy to have something it actually desired to wear. We wore those pink pajamas for three years until they were in tatters.

I've had many experiences like that with my body, and they have gone beyond what my body would like to eat or what it would like to wear. Once you reconnect with your body, it will give you information about all kinds of things. I was once at the airport waiting to go to Europe; we had boarded a plane and we were all set to go when they announced over the loudspeaker that there was something wrong and all the passengers had to disembark and go to another gate to board a different plane. My body began to direct me in the form of an energetic awareness, and I followed that energy. It was saying, "Go here, go there. Don't do that. Go to the desk now." My body knew what we needed to do to get a comfortable seat on the new flight, which was on a smaller plane that had fewer seats with decent legroom, and because I followed the energy, I got one of those seats.

These are just a few examples of the ways I've reconnected with my body. Since then, I've assisted many people who had addiction issues in the same process of reconnecting with their bodies.

Listening to the Experts

Sometimes people tell me they are connected with their body, but what they usually mean is they've listened to a diet expert, an exercise expert or a clothing expert in order to learn what they needed to impose on their body. Something like ninety percent of diet and exercise regimes fail. Why is that? Because they're about imposing someone else's point of view on *your* body. And how much do you judge yourself as a failure because you've tried this diet, exercise regime, skin care regime or whatever it was for you, and it didn't work?

Now that I listen to my body, I don't have to impose anybody else's point of view on it. I don't need diets. Sometimes my body will say, "Could you cut down on the carbs a little bit?" It's not so much a voice; it's an awareness.

If you connect with your body, it will let you know what it requires. What if you never had to depend on an expert again? Would you be willing to choose that now? Every time you listen to what an expert says is right for you without consulting your body, you diminish yourself and your knowing, and you put yourself back in the energy of addiction where the answer is always outside yourself. You once again make yourself less.

I'm not saying that you shouldn't listen to what people say or that you should disregard the information you receive. My point is that you don't need to make anyone else an "expert" and ignore your body. For example, your body might tell you, "You need to go to the doctor." So, you go to the doctor and she tells you ten things you need to do. You sit there nodding your head up and down saying, "Uh-huh, uh-huh, yes, Doctor."

You don't say, "I'm sorry, Doctor, my body doesn't agree with the fifth thing," because she'll think you're nuts. Just say, "Thank you so much." Remember, in general, the doctor is depending on other so-called experts. She's not going with what she knows, either.

143

When you leave the doctor's office, ask your body, "Body, of those ten things she told us, which ones are going to work for you?"

Your body may say, "One, three, and seven. The rest don't work for me."

You say, "Okay."

When you go back to the doctor and she asks, "How did those things work out for you?" you can reply, "One, three, and seven worked very well, the rest not so much." You don't have to say, "I didn't do them." Just play it according to what works for the situation, and underneath it all, you'll know that you listened to your body.

How Do You Treat Your Body?

If your body were another person you were very close to, how would you act toward that person? Would you be grateful for him or her? Would you listen to your friend? Would you acknowledge how wonderful he was? Would you take him as he was and maybe ask him questions about what would improve his life or what he would like? Or would you be critical and try to get him to change by telling him he was wrong here and stupid there?

This is the way we've been taught to treat our bodies. Very few people say, "You're a great body. Thank you for being with me and supporting me and doing all these wonderful things with me."

When you first begin to communicate with your body after a long period of ignoring it, you may receive a hostile response. Consider this in the light of a friend you've treated badly for years. If you suddenly call her and say, "I'd really like to be your friend," she might be hesitant or suspicious about resuming a relationship with you. You may wish to apologize to your body for ignoring it and treating it so carelessly. You can say, "Body, I'm sorry I've treated you so badly for so long. Please give me another chance. Let's see if we can get on the right track together." Your body can actually be your best friend. It makes the best friend possible, because guess what? You're always together.

When you allow your body to become your best friend, you are one step closer to walking away from any kind of addictive or compulsive behavior, because bodies don't care for those kinds of behaviors. In fact, I've never known anyone who was completely at home with his or her body who engaged in any addictive or compulsive behavior. Those behaviors just don't happen when you are connected to and with your body—and your body will support you coming to a place of choice.

Arbitrary Standards for Bodies

Many of the people I work with fall into the trap of trying to make their body fit into the current arbitrary standards for what a body should look like. If you're a female, you're made to believe you need to be thin. If you're a male, it's okay to have a little bit more weight as long as you're bulked up and have muscles. It's never about accepting your body and celebrating it; it's always about getting you to find what's wrong with your body so you can buy a program, a book, a food, a supplement or an exercise video. Or maybe it's about getting plastic surgery or botox injections so you fit in and finally become happy with the way you look, which of course, you never will, because you'll find something else that's wrong with your body.

Your Body Knows How It Wants to Look

Your body actually knows what it wants to look like. There is a size and shape it would like to be. Are you imposing somebody else's ideal on your body? If you are, I encourage you to stop right now. This may sound strange to you, but you can ask your body what it wishes to look like, and it will let you know. Just say, "Body, show me what you wish to look like." It may not respond immediately, but if you're willing to keep asking and be aware, one day when you're walking on a trail, someone will pass you, and your body will say, "That!" Or one evening when you're watching TV, your body will say, "There!"

Let your body know that you're willing to allow it to be the size and shape it desires to be and to work with it to achieve that. Imagine for a moment what it would be like to have a body that feels wonderful, beautiful and happy with itself. Is it necessarily going to look like what fashion magazines have defined as the perfect body? Maybe not, but you're going to feel so good, it won't matter. And the happier and more connected you are with your body, the less you will be drawn to engage in addictive or compulsive behavior.

A Non-Judgmental View of Your Body

I invite you to try taking a different perspective on your body. If you were looking at your body through a cat's eyes or a dog's eyes, which are the eyes of no judgment, what would you see? Would the cat be thinking, "Oh wow! Your butt is so big!" or "I can't believe you don't have any pecs!" or "Ew, you've got a lot of wrinkles!" I don't think so.

One of the reasons that it is so easy to be around animals is that they have absolutely no judgments about bodies. Can you imagine a lizard sunning itself on a rock and saying, "My belly is disproportionate to my tail. I really ought to do something about that"? There is so much allowance and gratitude for bodies in nature. And let me point out: Addiction does not exist in nature. It's a human creation.

Pain

When I talk about bodies, people often ask me, "What about pain? I have a lot of pain."

Do you suppose that pain might be one of the ways the body

gets in touch with you, especially if you've been ignoring it for years? I've found that pain is the body's last resort when it doesn't know what else to do. It tries to get your attention with a feather-light touch and you say, "No, I didn't feel anything, uh-uh." Then it shoves you a bit, and you say, "That was uncomfortable, but I think I'll go ahead and do some exercise or go help this friend again or drink some more, anything to distract me from my body. I'm not going to pay attention to that little shove."

Finally your body resorts to giving you pain because you didn't listen to its more subtle communications. Pain is your body's way of getting your attention. When you have what's called pain—and I encourage you to use the word *intensity* instead, because that takes away the negative connotation—ask:

"Hey, Body, what awareness are you giving me that I've been unwilling to receive?"

You may not get an answer right away, but if you continue to use that question, you'll eventually allow yourself to have that awareness.

Recently I created a great deal of neck pain—or intensity—in my neck. Why do I say I created it? Because I hadn't been willing to listen to the subtle signs from my body. By the time the intensity was great, I knew I had to start asking questions and listening to my body's response. When I finally asked my body about what was going on, I realized I had not been willing to allow it to have the energy and support it required to keep up with everything I had been doing. When I changed my habits and became willing to take my body into consideration again, the intensity disappeared.

If you are experiencing intensity in your body, I encourage you to keep asking questions. At some point, you'll have an awareness of what you might do to change the situation. Does that mean that you don't use medication or have it checked out by a doctor? No.

But there is almost always something else you can do to speed your recovery and greatly diminish the intensity you are experiencing.

Taking Things out of Other Bodies

I had a client with an addiction to alcohol that was not clearing. We worked together for about six weeks, and nothing was moving, which was very unusual. Finally I asked her, "Whose addiction is this, anyway?"

She looked startled, and then answered, "Oh! It's my mother's." She never had a problem with alcohol again!

The same can be true for arthritis, headaches or almost anything that's going on with a body. This isn't difficult to understand if you remember that everything is energy. Your body is energy. The table is energy. Thoughts, feelings and emotions are energy. Addiction is an energy. The body can take all these forms of energy out of other people's bodies.

So, when you perceive something happening in your body, you're well-advised to ask, "Is this mine—or someone else's?" or "Who does this belong to?" If you discover that it's not yours, return it to sender. You aren't helping other people by taking on their illness or physical condition. You don't heal their pain by taking it on. When you take it on, it's still present for them on some kind of energetic level, but they can't heal it either because you've taken it away from them. Returning it to sender benefits everyone.

Eating and Bodies

I have a program called, "Are You Eating to Live or Living to Eat?" Most people who sign up for this program are aware that they don't have a very happy relationship with their body; most of them are fighting with it all the time. There's a nasty cycle in place that goes like this: They want a piece of chocolate cake, so they eat a piece of chocolate cake, then they get angry at themselves for eating it. Then, in order to avoid the bad feelings they've created by judging themselves, they go back and have another piece of chocolate cake.

At the beginning of this program, I ask class participants what they would like to get out of the program, and most them say, "I'd like to lose weight." Just a few say they'd like to have a better relationship with their body. At the end of the program, I ask, "Are you happy with the results you got?" It's amazing how people respond. Instead of saying, "I feel great about my body because I've lost weight," they almost unanimously reply with statements like, "I have lost some weight, but that doesn't really matter to me any more. My relationship with my body has changed so much. I don't judge it as harshly. I now rejoice in my body, and we're having so much fun. We went swimming yesterday and we played with the kids. My body lets me know what to eat now, and slowly I can see the way it's changing. I stand up taller. I'm getting more fit. I'm much more aware of the world of my five senses. I'd still like to drop some pounds, but that is not what occupies my attention anymore. It's about having gratitude for my body and working with it in a way that honors both of us."

Your body is always a participant to some degree in your addictive or compulsive behavior. The body, like the natural world, doesn't actually resonate with addiction or compulsion. You have to detach from it and override it in order to force its participation in the addiction. The more you are in touch with your body and the more you honor it, the more it will assist you in moving beyond your addictive or compulsive behavior.

Some Things You Can Do to Nurture Your Body

Here are some things my clients and I have found to be nurturing to our bodies. You will probably have your own items to add to this list, so please continue to ask your body what would be nurturing to it. Your body is always changing so it may have different responses each time you ask.

Hugs

Hugs, real hugs, are very nourishing to a body. I'm not talking about tent hugs where you're standing far apart and kind of leaning in towards the other person to pat him or her on the back. Those hugs don't feel like much of anything. And I'm not talking about stiffening up so it's like hugging a stone statue. Nor am I talking about a hug that's an excuse for someone to grope your body. I'm talking about a hug that's a genuine connection between two bodies. There is so much care, connection and nurturance. It's true gifting and receiving for your body.

Massage

Massage can be another way to gift to your body. Ask your body, "Would you like a massage or some other form of bodywork?" If it does, ask it to show you the bodyworker it would like to have. Don't immediately go to, "This is the most popular bodyworker in my area," or "This is the cheapest one." Ask your body, "Who would you like to go and see?" If it's a lot of money, say to your body, "I'm happy to take you to this bodyworker, but I need some assistance in generating the money." Your body can help you do that. Your body is amazing at what it can bring into your life—but you have to connect with it. You have to ask it.

Access Consciousness® Bars*

Access Consciousness® Bars are a body process that can be incredibly nurturing to bodies. Many of my clients have found that

_____

*You can locate an Access Bars® or Body Facilitator near you through the Access Consciousness® website provided at the back of the book.

they have less desire to engage in their addictive or compulsive behavior after just a few Bars sessions.

The person receiving the Bars usually lies on a massage table, and the facilitator gently places his or her hands on thirty-two different points on the person's head. This releases a lot of the "trash" your body has taken on—the thoughts, feelings and emotions you've picked up from other people. It's kind of like deleting files on your computer. At worst, you'll feel like you had a good massage; at best, you'll open the door to changing your life.

Access Consciousness® Body Processes*

There are many amazing body processes offered by Access Consciousness® body facilitators. If you're interested in finding our about them, you can check the Access Consciousness® website for facilitators and classes in your area.

Smiles

Smiling is another very simple and effective thing you can do. In its natural state, your body is happy. It likes to smile—and smiling can have many positive effects on your body. It can lower blood pressure, release endorphins and relieve stress. I highly encourage you to smile more.

There are many other exercises and activities you can do to help you get in touch with, nurture and care for your body. I invite you to explore this area and see how much greater your connection with your body can be.

---

*You can locate an Access Consciousness® Body Facilitator near you through the Access Consciousness® website: www.accessconsciousness.com.

CHAPTER NINE

Addiction and Past Lives

*No one thing is the cause of your addiction, and no one thing is the
answer to it, but past lives may be playing a role in your continuing
addictive or compulsive behavior.*

In my work with addiction over the last twenty-plus years, I have
encountered people who have tried again and again to clear their
addictive or compulsive behavior but were unable to do so until I
asked them about past lives.

At the outset, I want to say that looking at past lives can be a *factor* in enabling people to walk away from their addictions. Past lives
are never, in and of themselves, the *cause* of addiction. Ultimately,
moving beyond an addiction comes down to your willingness to
have more of you and to make the choices that allow you to be more
aware and more present in your life.

In this chapter, I'd like to talk about some of my clients who
were able to move on from their addictions after we cleared a past
life connection with their addictive or compulsive behavior. There
is absolutely no requirement for you to believe in past lives. All I'm
asking you to do is to consider using a tool like heavy or light to see
if this is something that might apply to you.

Eating Disorders and Past Lives

Before I found the tools of Access Consciousness®, I chose to not take clients with eating disorders into my psychotherapy practice because there was such a low rate of success in treating them. Even with extensive psychotherapy, people who are bulimic or anorexic or who binge on food are commonly told they will struggle with their condition for the rest of their lives and will probably never get over it. They are often hospitalized, monitored and put on strict regimens with food, but none of that really works. These actions are a way of managing people's symptoms rather giving them tools, information and processing that will allow them to come out of the behavior. It was painful for me to work with people who had no real hope for recovery, so I chose not to work with individuals who had disordered relationships with food.

The tools of Access Consciousness® gave me a way to approach these disorders that had to do with undoing past life decisions, judgments and conclusions that were holding the behavior in place. After I had been using these tools for only a short time, I received a call from a woman in her forties who had been bulimic since her teens. She asked me if I would work with her. She told me she had tried psychotherapy but she hadn't had a good result. I said, "I've never seen anyone have a great deal of success with the kind of eating disorder you have. I can't promise anything, but I have some tools, techniques and information from Access Consciousness® if you are interested in trying them."

She said, "Let's give it a try," so we did, and in four one-hour sessions, she was free from bulimia, and she has not binged or purged since that time. What's important about this story is that her particular eating issues were tied into a past life. As we worked together, we discovered that over 2,000 years ago, she had been involved in the murder of someone she knew to be innocent. She carried forward enormous amounts of guilt that required her to continuously punish herself by depriving her body of sustenance. When she was able to destroy and uncreate the decisions and judgments she made about herself in the past life, it changed everything for her in the present.

I have found that for many people with eating disorders, the disordered relationship with food serves as a punishment of the being and the body for what they considered to be a heinous crime committed in a past life. I've also had many clients realize that starvation or food deprivation in a past life was one of the main factors behind their need to stuff their pantries, their refrigerators and their bodies.

Smoking

The decision that one needs to be punished for actions in a past life can also play a role in other addictive or compulsive behaviors. For instance, I worked with a man who had been a smoker all of his adult life, despite innumerable attempts to stop. After we tried a number of interventions but with no real results, I asked him, "Truth, are there past lives involved here?"

He said yes and he looked at something he believed he had done. It was an act he had judged as so terrible that he decided he did not have the right to breathe. He was smoking in this lifetime as a way to cut off his breath and slowly kill himself in punishment for that act. Once he was able to re-examine his decision, he lost his compulsion to smoke.

Being a Victim and Encouraging Abuse

I've also asked about past lives when people seemed determined to be a victim and encourage abuse. I am not saying this is true in all cases, but if people seem to be continually inviting abusive treatment, there may be a past life incident that prompts them to believe they need to be punished.

I recently spoke with a woman who told me that everyone in her life was abusive to her, even people who were generally kind to others. After we talked about how she created that behavior in others, I asked, "Are you punishing yourself for something you did in a past life?"

She said, "Yes."

I asked, "What was it?"

She said, "I killed my entire family."

I asked, "At some point did all of them kill you?"

She said, "Yes, they did."

I asked, "Can you see that we've all been and done everything?"

Once she had that awareness and was able to come out of what she described as karmic debt, she was able to let go of her constant creation of abusive situations.

All of us have been everything and done everything. You have been a king and a queen and a slave; you've been a guru and a follower; you've been a nobody and a somebody; you've been a pauper and you've been wealthy beyond your imagination. You've been a victim of crimes and abuse and you've been a perpetrator of crimes and abuse. If you can give up the judgment of what you've been and done, it can give you enormous freedom. It can free you from the need to punish yourself or others and give you the space to be present and show up as you.

Relationship Addiction

Past lives also show up in cases of relationship addiction. Have you ever seen someone across a crowded room and thought, "That's the one. I've found my prince or my princess"? Usually that kind of reaction indicates you have had a lot of lives with that person. And you may have made a load of vows, commitments, contracts and agreements with him or her on the order of, "I'll love you forever," "We'll always be together," or "I will always take care of you." You may want to look at this person and ask, "Is this actually my prince or princess? Or is this someone that I was attached to in a past life?"

That attachment could have been positive, but perhaps it was negative. I worked with a client who could not disconnect from his very abusive ex. She had been incredibly cruel to him. She stole his money. She demeaned him. She did all kinds of nasty things, and he would say, "But I love her. I don't know why, but I need to be with her."

First of all, "loving somebody" is never a reason to be with anyone, especially when that person treats you badly. The reason to be with someone is that he or she expands and contributes to your life.

I asked my client, "Is being with this woman expansive to you?"

He said, "No, actually, she is destroying me, but I feel so addicted to her that I don't know what to do. I can't move on."

As we began to look at what was going on, I asked him, "Is there a past life involved in this?"

He said, "Yes, absolutely. Many, many, many."

I asked, "So, what's your awareness here?"

He replied, "She saved my life many times, so I owe it to her, no matter how badly she treats me, to stay with her and do whatever she wants me to do. I am her slave."

I said, "Something about that feels really heavy. Let me ask you a question. Is it actually true that she saved you all those times?"

He paused, looked at it, and said, "No, those were lies that she implanted in me."

Once he spotted the lies, he was able to move past them. His addiction to this relationship fell like a house of cards. The lie was the bottom card, and once we pulled it out, everything tumbled down. He told me in his last session, "I don't even think about her any more." He had begun to direct his energy toward creating his life.

Here's the thing that is so interesting. He could have gone the other way. He could have decided that the karma and the trauma-drama of those past life incidents were real, and gotten stuck in them forever. But he didn't do that. He simply let it all go. It fell away, and now he is free of it. But even if my client's ex had saved him all those times, that was her choice. He didn't owe her anything.

Here is another thing to consider: How many "until death do us part" contracts and commitments do you have with all the people you have been married to or enslaved to? You make contracts with people, and because the being never actually dies, the agreements you made millions of years ago may be running and ruining your life now. You may wish to destroy and uncreate all those oaths, vows, fealties, swearings, comealties, contracts, agreements and commitments. They have no place in your life now.

Living in the present is being with each person in your life in the now and having a choice about what you are going to do in each ten seconds. Can you get the energy of that? How light is it?

Compulsively Assisting Others

Past commitments can also be at work when people feel a strong need to assist others. In the past you may have made commitments in religious orders or other groups, and you may feel you've let people down or been the cause of their destruction by not following through on your promises. If you notice that there is a compulsive quality in relation to trying to help someone or solve their problems, or if you feel you *must* assist them and that's your role in life, you may wish to ask whether past lives are involved.

Unchanging Situations

Any time you are stuck in a situation that doesn't seem to change despite having used many different tools or approaches, I encourage you to ask, "Are past lives involved here?" You can also ask:

- Am I punishing myself for something?
- Am I making up for a behavior I've judged as damaging?
- Am I fulfilling a commitment I made in another lifetime?

If you get a yes, ask some more questions. All of us, at some time or another, have bought into the idea of cause and effect, karma, and some kind of, "I did this to them, so now I owe them," or "They did that to me, and now they owe me." None of that is true. That kind of thinking creates polarity and prevents you and others from moving into a space of consciousness and awareness.

Consciousness includes everything and judges nothing. When you are operating from a space of consciousness, the behavior that comes from that space is generative and creative, not destructive and contractive.

There is another point I'd like to make about seeing oneself or another as the cause of "damage" or "destruction". Those concepts are a judgment. All behavior is essentially neutral from the point of view that the observer makes a judgment about whether it's good or bad. If things were intrinsically good or bad, every observer would make the same judgment and see things in the same way. And we know that's not the case.

Is This Relevant Now?

Coming out of addictive and compulsive behavior is about being present in the now. You don't need to distract yourself by trying to figure out the past or by going through all kinds of distortions to make up for damage you may or may not have caused. If you're doing that, you are living in the past. You are in your head; you are not in your awareness. You are not present, and you are not going to be able to move forward.

One of the things that keeps us stuck in the past is the idea of forgiveness. Please remember that forgiving keeps you in the polarity of right and wrong. It always involves a judgment. What if you didn't owe anyone anything and no one owed you anything? What would it be like to move into a space of letting everything be? When you experience a charge or a memory or a thought comes up—you can always ask, "Is that relevant now?"

Discovering and then clearing a past life connection to your addictive or compulsive behavior can bring almost immediate relief and a freedom you might never have dreamed possible.

CHAPTER TEN

Addiction and Entities

Everything is conscious.
Once you're willing to be aware of that,
your life will expand in ways you can't even imagine.

Entities can have a very powerful effect on addiction and recovery. This is a topic that is rarely discussed to the detriment of many people who are trying to rid themselves of addictive or compulsive behavior.

Most people think of entities as beings that don't have bodies, like ghosts or spirits; those are definitely examples of entities, but the definition of *entity* includes much more than that. In the broadest sense, an entity is simply an energy with an identity. You're an entity and I'm an entity. Animals are entities. Houses, chairs and businesses are entities. If you write a song, that song becomes an entity in and of itself. There are, of course, also entities who don't have bodies, and they too, are simply an energy with an identity.

One of the biggest mistakes people make is to assume that only human beings are conscious. It's an assumption of superiority that can create enormous limitation in our lives because it renders us unwilling to receive information other entities are giving us, whatever form they take. If you have decided that most of the things and beings in the universe are not aware and not willing to gift to you,

you won't be able to receive from them. It's like deciding that only brown-haired, forty-three year old white males have anything to offer you. The truth is that everything is conscious. And once you're willing to know that and receive that, your life will expand in ways you can't even imagine.

Unfortunately, the idea that only human beings are conscious has been perpetuated by some religions and churches that teach that human beings are superior to everything else on the planet. Check this idea out for yourself. Is that true? Say to yourself, "Only human beings are conscious." Heavy or light? Unless you were taught this idea and unquestioningly bought it, I'll bet that statement is heavy for you, which means it's a lie. What is true is that we are all part of consciousness and oneness, which is why we can communicate with entities of all kinds.

You may ask, "What does all of this have to do with addiction?" It has a lot to do with addiction for a couple of reasons: First, once you become aware that everything is conscious, it allows you to participate in the gifting and receiving of everything in the universe. Second, if you're unwilling to be aware of the presence of entities and their influence upon your addictive or compulsive behavior, you may become the effect of them and what they would like you to do.

Entities Who Do Not Have a Physical Form

I recently did some research on the Internet and discovered that fifty to eighty percent of the people in the U.S.A. have had an experience with a being that didn't have a physical body. These people had a deceased loved one show up or they had an experience with what might be called a ghost, spirit guide, angel or demon. I want you to know that you're not alone if you've had some kind of experience with a being who did not have a physical form. You are actually in the majority. It's very helpful to know that not only can you be aware of entities that do not have bodies, but by increasing your awareness and understanding of them, you can add more ease to your life.

Many people assume that beings who do not have a body are always wise, truthful and spiritual. Please don't make that mistake. If your Aunt Jane was an idiot when she was alive, she's still going to be an idiot when she comes to talk to you without her body. Entities also lie. Have you heard people say, "I channel the Archangel Michael, Jesus or some other ancient wise one"? Do you think that entities don't have fun fooling beings in bodies? Any time an entity shows up and tells you who it is, don't make the mistake of assuming that it's telling you the truth or that it knows more than you do.

Beings without bodies can show up anywhere. They can occupy any space. They can be in your house, in your car or in your computer. They can occupy your body or the area around it. They can also occupy animals' bodies. These beings are in varying states of awareness, and many of them don't realize they've had other lifetimes. They may not be aware they lost their body centuries ago.

When these entities are present but unrecognized, they can have a detrimental effect on you, your body and your life, and in some cases, they can exacerbate your addictive or compulsive behavior or make recovering from an addiction more difficult. However, please do not make the mistake of blaming entities for your addictive behavior or seeing them as the cause of it. They may be a factor that influences your actions, but they didn't cause the addiction, nor can they fix it.

Entities and Addictions

Years ago, I had a client who was concerned about the amount she was drinking. Initially she drank to deal with social anxiety, and over time, she began to get more and more and more depressed. The depression seemed extreme to me. She had unexpected crying jags and thoughts of suicide. After exploring many possible causes,

I asked if there was an entity involved. My client immediately felt lighter. The answer was a definite yes. This particular entity had attached to her during an alcoholic blackout. It had been a person who committed suicide with alcohol and pills and it was attracted to my client because she drank. Once we cleared the entity, my client's depression greatly lessened and we continued our work to move her beyond using alcohol in an addictive or compulsive way.

Another one of my clients was a woman who was having a very difficult time losing weight. We used a variety of tools, but no change was occurring. Finally I asked about entities. It turned out that my client had an entity who had starved to death, and it was using her to overeat in an attempt to mitigate its memories of starving. Once we cleared the entity, my client began to make progress with losing weight.

In my work with addictions, I've often found that a person's cravings can be created by entities that have the same addiction as the person whose body they inhabit. Even though the entity no longer has a body, it is still interested in acting out its addiction, and it attempts to do so through the person. For instance, there are entities who desire to smoke, and they attach themselves to people who smoke. A particular tip-off that an entity is driving the desire is when you hear, "*You* need a drink now," or "*You* should light up a joint." When this occurs, you can be assured that the craving belongs to an entity, because you would not refer to yourself as "you."

Relapse

In traditional treatment programs, alcohol is often described as "cunning, baffling, and powerful" because the desire to drink seems to overtake people randomly, even after they've been practicing their program for a period of time. I've found that acting out with an addictive or compulsive behavior often occurs when an entity is involved.

When someone comes in and says something like, "I was doing really well in my recovery, but I relapsed last night. I don't understand what was going on," I am immediately alerted that entities may be involved. Interestingly, once they are cleared, what is termed "relapse" in traditional programs rarely occurs, unless the person has not yet cleared their primary addiction to judgment and wrongness.

What Opens You up to Entities Without Bodies?

As I've said, one of the things that invites entities into your life is engaging in addictive or compulsive behavior. Why would that be? Because when you engage in that behavior you basically check out and put a "for rent" sign on your body. This makes sense if you remember that addiction is the place you go where you don't exist. It's a place where you're not being present. And any time you're not being present, you open up the space for entities to come in and occupy your body.

Many years ago, before I knew about entities and addiction, I had a very dear friend I will call John. John had problems with alcohol. He had been sober for a while, but he could not make his life work. He started drinking heavily again—a couple of fifths of vodka a day—and he basically made the choice to die. I offered to assist him if he ever wanted help with his addiction, but at some point, I chose not to be around him any more because there was so little of him present to relate to and it was very clear that he had no interest in changing his behavior.

One day a mutual friend went over to John's house to bring him some food. She told me that she knocked on the door and called, "John, John, where are you?" Finally she let herself into the house, and a being came out of the living room. It was John's body, but it was clearly not John. It had a very forceful, violent, destructive energy. She told me the face did not even look like John's face. She kept saying, "John, John, come out." The body finally shook and John became present. He was a very kind and generous person whose energy was completely different from the being she had first seen.

The fact is, that entity could not have entered John's body if John had not made the choice to absent himself and his body by consuming enormous amounts of alcohol. The more he chose the path of self-destruction, the more he opened the door to these darker forces. Sadly, John was determined to end his life and he didn't change the direction he was heading.

There is no reason to fear entities. They don't have any power over you that you don't give them. They cannot force themselves on you. You are not going to be possessed unless you invite them in. I relate this story about John because it's a dramatic example of what you can create when you choose to not be present in your life. When you participate in any compulsive or addictive behavior, you can invite in destructive entities who also had that addiction when they were alive. If you've ever seen someone make a huge personality change when they were very drunk or completely engaged in any other addictive behavior, it's likely that he or she vacated their body and another entity came in.

Clearing Entities

Entities can be cleared using processes from Access Consciousness®. There may be other ways to clear them as well. I encourage you to ask questions and do what works for you.

A final note: Please remember that no entity can take you over unless you allow it to. And no entity is larger or more powerful than you, even those who choose to call themselves demons. You are the one who is in charge of your life and your body. You may require some assistance, but if you so choose, you can clear any entity who is adversely affecting you.

When we are used to having our lives run by an addictive or compulsive behavior, it begins to feel natural and comfortable to make ourselves the effect of other people, places and things. Some people even feel very "special" when they realize they have entities. Please don't make this mistake. You are valuable for who you truly are, for the uniqueness of you and the gift you can be to the world. Making yourself the effect of any entity is denying yourself—and the possibility of a truly great life.

CHAPTER ELEVEN

What Is True Recovery?

*People in true recovery have come to a space of choice
with their addictive or compulsive behavior. There is no sense of
having to engage in it—or having to resist engaging in it.*

In most traditional addiction treatment programs, being in recovery means you are no longer engaging in a designated addictive or compulsive behavior. But because these programs address only the secondary addiction and give no attention to the primary addiction, many people end up trading a less acceptable addiction like drinking alcohol for a more socially acceptable one like compulsively working—or even attending recovery meetings. They're still looking for an addictive or compulsive behavior to escape into and relieve the pain of the wrongness of them—the self-judgment, the sense of not fitting in and the feeling of being overwhelmed by the thoughts and feelings of others.

Most traditional recovery programs require participants to use a prescribed set of steps on a continuing basis as a means and measure of their recovery. It's seen as a lifelong requirement for keeping the addictive behavior at bay. This way of approaching recovery presents it as a kind of remission from addiction. It's as if the symptoms of a disease are present but they are being managed by the steps you perform so you can return to being the person you used to be and having the life you used to have.

Through all the years I participated in conventional recovery programs, it never seemed to me that not drinking, not smoking or not engaging in my other habitual behaviors was enough. Even though I was aware that not engaging in these behaviors would open up more possibility for me—I wouldn't be hung over, I would have more physical capacity with my lungs—I never liked the idea that the possibility of addiction would always be lurking in the background as something I was powerless over and that I would be remanded to a lifelong program.

I've always thought that recovery had to be about much more than that. As the concepts of Right Recovery for You began to come together, I started to look more deeply into what true recovery could actually be. In this chapter, I'd like to present some of the elements of true recovery as I see it.

As you read, I encourage you to make notes about what your recovery would look like for you, because it can be something different for each person. As you come to a greater awareness of what recovery is for you, you will be able to make it a more achievable target for yourself. This is important, because if you don't know what recovery is for you, you can't have a target that's reachable. You won't recognize it when it shows up. Say, for example, that you wished to have more abundance in your life but you didn't define what abundance was. How would you know what to shoot for? And how would you know when you had it? It's the same for true recovery. You need to know what you're aiming for. This does not mean that your concepts and targets won't change as you grow and choose what's expansive for you. It's simply something you start with to give you direction.

Destroy and Uncreate Everything You Have Decided Recovery Is

Before I begin to talk about what true recovery might look like, I would like to invite you to destroy and uncreate everything you've ever been told or decided that recovery is—or isn't. If you're approaching your recovery with any of the conventional misconceptions, rigid beliefs or definitions of what recovery means, you're going to limit what's possible for you.

After you've destroyed and uncreated all the ideas about recovery that you accepted, believed or went into agreement with, I invite you to consider the following possibilities:

- What if true recovery isn't about a state of abstinence but rather an ongoing process of asking questions, looking at possibilities and making choices that allow your life to expand in ways you never dreamed were possible?

- What if true recovery is about becoming aware of the energy of what you would like your current and future life to be, then choosing to be that energy?

- What if true recovery is about choosing consciousness?

Consciousness

That last question raises a key point: What if true recovery is about choosing consciousness? A lot of people talk about consciousness, but the only person I know who has really defined it is Gary Douglas. Gary says, "Consciousness includes everything and judges nothing." Addiction is included in your universe, but it's not something you have to choose.

When you choose consciousness, all possibilities are available to you. When you choose addiction, unconsciousness and anti-consciousness are your only choices. True recovery is about having all possibilities available to you—not limiting yourself and your awareness. Choosing consciousness allows you to make choices from a much greater and more expanded field of awareness.

Most everyone is familiar with the energy and patterns of addiction—that contracted, limited, I-don't-exist space. But not everyone recognizes the energy of consciousness or true recovery, so I'd like to talk about some of the choices you may wish to make if you're interested in moving into true recovery.

The choice to be aware requires you to stay out of fantasy, unrealistic hopes or dwelling in the past or future. It is the willingness to stay present with yourself and others and whatever information is coming to you. While that may seem like an overwhelming target at first, it allows you to have much more control in your life. You can only choose something if you're willing to acknowledge that it's there in the first place.

Closely related to that is **the choice not to avoid anything.** I'm not talking about going around a pothole or getting out of town if a bad hurricane is coming. That's common sense. What I'm talking about is the willingness to face whatever comes your way rather than turning to an addictive or compulsive behavior to deal with what you have decided is too much to cope with. The great thing about the choice to not avoid anything is that when you choose it, you find you are actually much more competent and powerful than you've led yourself to believe.

The choice to have an internal frame of reference. When you have an internal frame of reference, you are not at the effect of others around you. You operate as the creative source in your life rather than the effect of what shows up. You are not concerned with what others think of you nor are you concerned with following accepted roles, patterns of behavior or the shoulds and oughts that so many people operate from. Instead, by being present and choosing what works for you, you can lead a life that is uniquely your own. This doesn't mean you are not aware of others or what they require or desire of you. It's not about being the lone ranger. It simply means that you are willing to be you no matter what pressures others are putting on you.

The choice to know what you know and to act from that space is closely related to having an internal frame of reference. It is about trusting yourself rather than looking outside of yourself for answers. It does not mean that you don't ask for or take in information. It does mean that you trust yourself to know what's true for you and to take appropriate action based on that knowing.

The choice to own that you've created everything in your life and that things didn't "just happen to you." This does not mean you are responsible for other people's behavior or that you haven't experienced abuse or other traumatic events in your life—but it does mean that you are responsible for your reactions and whatever actions you choose to take. People who see themselves as helpless victims of something that "just happened to them" often stay stuck in the victim mode forever and they're rarely able to move beyond their addictive or compulsive behavior.

I'm often asked why some people are able to move past their addictions and others are not. A big factor is their willingness to admit that addiction didn't happen to them; they made the choices that led to their addictive or compulsive behavior. That's actually good news, because if you made the choices that led to your addictive behavior to begin with, you can make different choices that lead to your recovery.

The choice to be happy and joyful. It *is* actually a choice. If you believe you can only be happy if...or when..., you are once again making yourself the effect of circumstances. What if you chose to be happy right now? Can you get the energy of that? Can you see how you would invite and create different experiences than if you were being miserable? Some people believe that if a friend or family member is depressed or sick that it's wrong to be happy. But do you actually do them—or the world—a favor by matching their energy? If you're operating out of sadness and worry, can you be the gift you are when you're happy? The willingness to be happy is a huge contribution to the world, and it will also lead to a more expansive life for you.

Tool: How Does It Get Any Better Than This?*

Here's a question you can use in any circumstance to invite new possibilities into your life. Try it when anything positive or pleasant has occurred. Did you just get a promotion, do well on a test or leave for a lovely vacation? Ask, "How does it get any better than this?" You might be amazed at what shows up.

You can also use it when you've come to the conclusion that something is bad or terrible. Did you just sprain your ankle? Did a waitress spill hot coffee on you? Are you stuck in traffic? Asking, "How does it get any better than this?" allows you to see that something positive can come out of any event.

Recently I was driving by myself and got a flat tire on the highway. Rather than going to "Oh no! This is terrible!" I kept asking, "How does it get any better than this?"

Almost immediately, a police officer stopped and helped me change the tire. How does it get any better than *that*?

When you keep asking, "How does it get any better than this?" you become more open to receiving, and your life begins to show up differently.

It's also very useful when you're working with your addictive or compulsive behavior. Did you choose not to stop at the bar for a couple of drinks as usual before you went home? Did you choose to listen to your body and not have your normal second or third helping of food? Did you choose not to stay late at work for the fourth night in a row? Asking, "How does it get any better than this?" acknowledges the choices you've made that expand your life and invite even greater ease and choice in dealing with your addiction.

If you choose to engage in your addictive or compulsive behavior, asking, "How does it get any better than this?" opens up other possibilities. Many people believe that if they have one more sexual encounter that has a compulsive quality, they have to throw up their hands and have more and more. Or if they go out and compulsively overspend on new goodies again, they have to continue doing that. Asking, "How does it get any better than this?" creates a space that offers the opportunity to choose something different.

*"How does it get any better than this?" is an Access Consciousness® tool.

174

The choice to have allowance for yourself and others. Allowance is the willingness to have an "interesting point of view" for yourself and everyone and everything else. It's the willingness to be aware that people have choice and create their lives, and that it's not up to you to tell them what to do—or what not to do.

Allowance is different from acceptance. Acceptance implies a judgment. You've already decided that someone has done something bad or wrong but you're going to accept it anyway. It's a position of superiority. Allowance is a position of neutrality. Things are what they are; you don't judge them one way or another, which allows you to be aware of what is actually going on. You've moved beyond the dictates of right and wrong, good and bad, into a space of your own awareness and knowing. You trust in your knowing and there is a confidence that comes from being aware that you have the tools and the power to create the life you desire.

The choice to not tell or be run by stories. Stories are the way we justify and explain our's or other people's behavior: "I gamble because my mother did," "I am addicted to pornography because my father showed it to me when I was young," "My husband abuses me because he was abused as a child." Most of us embellish our stories to make them seem plausible, but stories are just stories. Not only are they not true, but if you believe your stories, you can't move on to change anything. The choice to not tell stories is also the choice to be present with what is, rather than using the past to explain why you are the way you are. All stories keep you in the energy of addiction.

(Please note that when I refer to stories, I'm not talking about giving real information. I often ask clients about their history with their addiction because it gives me facts and insights that can be very helpful to our work. The stories that are not helpful are those that are used either to divert or to offer reason and/or justification for the behavior.)

The choice to be vulnerable. Being vulnerable is often seen as a weakness. Actually, the opposite is true. It's a position of strength and courage. Total vulnerability is the willingness to drop all of your barriers and receive everything. It's the willingness not to act on preconceived ideas about what you will or will not receive. For example, have you decided that you will receive from this kind of person but not that kind of person? Have you decided that you will receive from the city but not the country? Have you decided that you will receive from books but not TV? It takes tremendous courage to drop your barriers, preconceived ideas and everything you've decided is right or wrong, and everything you have solidified in place—and simply receive it all without judgment. We tend to think that barriers keep us safe, but if we have barriers up, we prevent ourselves from receiving information, awareness and many other things that are crucial to our well being.

The choice to have gratitude for everyone and everything in your life. Gratitude is about seeing the contribution that every being or event brings to your life, even those you may have judged to be negative. This is not a Pollyanna approach. It's actually quite realistic. When I was first in recovery, I bemoaned the years I'd lost to alcohol; now I'm grateful for them. Without my own experience of addiction and various forms of recovery, I would not be doing the work I am doing and enjoying so much. Every being and every event can facilitate greater awareness for us if we allow it to. The willingness to be grateful creates an energy of ease, expansion and forward motion while regret and resentment lead to contraction, resistance and reaction.

The choice to be in communion with your body. True recovery requires you to have a celebratory connection with your body. If you're not connected with your body, you can't actually end addiction, because you won't be fully present. Bodies are always abused and neglected when we engage in addictive or compulsive behaviors.

176

Recovery must include the body in an honoring and caring way. Treated with kindness and consideration, your body can become your best friend and gift to you in ways you've never imagined.

The choice to act from *being* rather than *doing*. Many people try to prove their worth by *doing;* for instance, a woman might say, "I'm going to be a great mother. I'm going to bake cupcakes twice a week, enroll my kids in three after-school activities, and make sure they do at least two hours of homework a night." This is very different from *being*, because being a truly great mother is not about setting forth a list of predetermined actions. It will look different for each mother and each child. When you're truly *being* a great mom, you're reading the energy of your child and you're seeing what you can contribute. There are no fixed ideas about what that's supposed to look like or what you're supposed to do.

When you choose to act from *being* rather than *doing,* you allow your *doing* to come from reading the energy of a situation and seeing what you can contribute rather than using a predetermined *doing* to prove that you're *being* something. *Being* is about the energy and space you are willing to be. The more you show up as you, the more you are stepping into the energy of being.

The choice to function from question, choice, possibility and contribution.* People in true recovery are always in the question; they're not concerned with having answers. They know that answers limit and questions empower. When you ask questions, you receive an ongoing stream of information that creates new possibilities. Every choice you make also creates a new set of possibilities and offers new ways of being and receiving contribution.

This is in contrast to operating from decision, judgment, conclusion and automatic pilot. With those, everything is fixed, nailed

---

*"Functioning from question, choice, possibility and contribution" is an Access Consciousness® concept.

down and contracted. Functioning from question, choice, possibility and contribution opens the door to an expansive, joyful and ever-evolving life.

What Are You Willing to Choose?

True recovery is an ongoing process. It's ever-expanding and ever-changing. Remember, you are the antidote to addiction. The willingness to show up as you allows you to participate in a recovery that goes beyond what you may have imagined before. Any of these choices creates a space where it's difficult for addictive and compulsive behaviors to exist. Just by choosing one or two of them, you can begin to become more aware, shift your energy and create a whole new set of possibilities.

Please choose what works for you, know what you know, and have the courage to step out and be the gift you truly are.

Judgment Takes Many Forms

In chapter four, I talked about some of the more common ways that judgment shows up, but it also takes many less-obvious forms. If you're choosing to let go of judgment, it will be helpful to identify many of the more subtle ways judgment appears in your life—because judgment has so much to do with taking on addictive and compulsive behavior.

Conclusion	Determination
Belief	Definition
Conviction	Comparison
Decision	Competition
Purpose	Significance
Resolution	Shoulds, Ought To's and Obligations

Conclusion. Judgment frequently takes the form of conclusions. So, what does a conclusion look like? Often conclusions are interpretations of events. Let's say someone you know walks by you and doesn't wave or say hello. You might conclude, "She doesn't like me," or "There must be something wrong with me," or "I must have offended her."

Instead, what if you asked a question like, "What's going on with that person?" If you asked a question, you might see that she was having a bad day or that she didn't recognize you. A question could change everything. But most of us don't ask a question. We go straight to conclusion.

Or let's say you invest some money in a business and it doesn't work out the way you wanted it to. A conclusion would be, "Things never work out for me," or "I'm no good with money." Instead, what if you asked questions like, "What was I unwilling to be aware of about this? Is there some way to turn this around? Is this the way I should be investing—or can I do something different?"

When you ask a question, you move yourself out of conclusion—and into an awareness of different possibilities.

Belief. Another way that judgment shows up is in beliefs. A belief is something you've decided is true based on your experience. Or it could be something you've bought from an authority figure who told you it was true. A belief can be about anyone or anything at all, including yourself.

Have you adopted beliefs about yourself as a part of your identity? These might be things like, "I'm good at business. That's my greatest strength," or "I'm just not a creative person," or "I'm disorganized." Those beliefs are just another form of judgment—and they're something you want to let go of. You might be thinking, "That's hard! Those things seem so true. And who would I be without them?" Remember, a belief is a form of judgment, and a judgment has a charge, whereas an awareness does not. If you say, "I'm good in business," and there is no charge, it may be an awareness. It's very helpful to check out the energy of anything you are saying about yourself or another.

Letting go of the beliefs you have about yourself is a simple concept, but in practice it may take a while because we've been taught from the very beginning of our life to judge ourselves. And it's those judgments—those beliefs—that lock everything in place in our life. They don't give us any room to move.

Then there are all the beliefs that show up in connection with addiction: "Once an addict, always an addict," "Giving up addiction is a long and painful process," or "Addiction means there is something terribly wrong with me."

There are also the beliefs that seem to come from our experience. I've worked with men who have said things like, "All women are devious. They are going to betray you." And I've worked with women who have told me things like, "All men are abusive."

My response is always, "Really? What's that based on?"

The man or the woman in question then says something like, "I've been there. My wife betrayed me," or "I've been married three times, and in each case my partner was abusive to me. So that proves my point."

Beliefs based on your limited experience are detrimental to you—because your point of view creates your reality. If you've decided that all women will betray you or that all men are abusive, that is exactly what you will create in your life. You will always experience what you choose to believe.

We also take on the beliefs of our society, our culture, our country, and our religion. These are the root of prejudice. All women are _____, all men are _____, all people of color are _____, all Italians are _____, all Jews are _____. I encourage you to question every belief you have, regardless of where it came from, because every belief is a judgment in one form or another. Use questions like:

- Is this belief actually true for me?
- What do I know about this subject?
- Who did I buy this belief from?

- How does it serve me in my life? Or not serve me?
- Am I willing to let this belief go?
- Have I used this belief to define me and give me an identity?
- Do I have a judgment that if I let this belief go, I won't know who I am?

Questions take you beyond beliefs. They give you the freedom you're looking for because they will help you create new pathways and possibilities for yourself. Instead of buying a belief, ask, "Are there other possibilities here?"

Conviction. Convictions are especially firm or solidified beliefs that can have far-reaching effects on your life. Often we use convictions to organize our world; for example, "I can't quit my addictive behavior. I need it to survive." No matter what form convictions take, they always involve judgment. They exclude awareness and possibility, and they don't give you any place else to go because, as I've said, whenever you have a fixed point of view, nothing that doesn't match it can show up.

One of the tip-offs that something is a conviction is when people become very zealous about their point of view. They are *convinced* it's true. For example, if you have the conviction that addiction is the work of the devil, you have condemned yourself to create that as your reality. However, if you're willing to ask questions like: "Is addiction *really* the work of the devil? Or did I have some part in creating it? Can I clear it? What else can I do to move beyond this addiction? Where else could I get a different point of view or more information?" then you have the possibility of something else showing up in your life.

Decision. Decisions are always based on judgments. There's a big difference between *choosing* and *deciding*. Choice is open and expansive. Decision has a solidity to it. "I have decided I am going to do this." That's it. There's a sense of finality to it.

Decisions trap us, because once we make a decision, we think it has to stay in place. For instance, if you've *decided* to take a job, how free are you to be aware a month later that the job isn't working? How free are you to say, "You know what? I'm going to do something different."

There's something else about decisions. Decisions are often made through a process of analysis that employs the mind. You try to figure out whether you should take a job by analyzing the hours, the pay, the benefits and other factors—and you exclude your knowing and your awareness. You think that if you analyze everything correctly, you will arrive at the right decision. But has that kind of analysis ever worked for you? No. Why is that? Because figuring things out is all about judgment.

Not only that, but we tend to judge ourselves severely if we go against our decisions. For instance, if you start dating a man and decide he's the most wonderful guy in the world, and then two months later you become aware that he's actually very self-centered and thinks little of you, you might have a difficult time saying, "Wait a minute. I'm going to change my mind. I'm leaving him." Generally, people feel they have to stick with their decisions, but doing this makes the decision bigger and more important than their awareness of what's actually happening.

Instead of operating from decision, I encourage you to move into choice. Choice is about being present in each moment and seeing what's going to work for you. With choice, you get to choose and choose again. You can ask, "Is it expansive to take this job? Yes? Okay." Six months later you can ask, "Is it expansive to stay with this job? No? Okay." You can choose something else. How different is that from saying, "Well, I decided to take this job, so I'm going to stick with it forever even though it's not at all what I want"?

With choice, you can say, "I choose to go on this diet," and five days later you can say, "My body doesn't want to do this any more.

I'm going to make a different choice." Or you could go into decision and say, "This is a six-week program and I'm going to stick it out, even though I feel awful and my body's telling me it doesn't want to do it any more."

One of the only constants in life is change. Things change all the time, and yet there's a huge judgment in this reality that the measure of someone's mental health is consistency and commitment. We admire people who stick with things no matter what. "I have been married to the same person for sixty years." "I have lived in the same place for forty years." That's wonderful—if you love the person you're married to or the place you live in. But you don't honor a place, another person, yourself or anything else if you know something is not working and you act as if it is.

Decision keeps you contracted because it's based on judgment. Choice is based on awareness; it allows you to expand and to honor yourself and everyone and everything else—and choice will assist you in moving beyond addiction.

Purpose. Purpose is the reason something exists or is done, made or used. A lot of people say they want to have a life purpose. But how much judgment is involved in having a life purpose? And how much does that statement of your life purpose cut off your awareness and possibilities?

For example, if your life purpose is to be kind, you have made a judgment that being kind is the only appropriate behavior in any situation. What if someone is stealing from you and you've decided that it would be unkind to tell her she can't stay in your home or visit you? So, she keeps coming to your home and stealing from you and you keep saying to yourself, "Well, I have the purpose to be kind, so I can't ask her to leave."

Do you see how having a life purpose could limit you? When you have a life purpose, you aren't able to be aware and to choose moment by moment. It doesn't allow you to have true freedom. Instead of having a life purpose, I encourage you to have priorities. They are not set in stone. If you make it a priority (rather than a purpose) to be kind, you can be aware in every situation and say, "My priority is to be kind here. What would that look like?" Maybe being kind in the situation where someone is stealing from you means being kind to yourself and telling the person she is no longer welcome in your house because you're aware she's stealing from you.

I invite you to move from purpose to priority, because purpose involves enormous amounts of judgment and it will lock you up the same way addictive behavior does.

Resolution. A resolution is like a goal; it's the object or end that you strive to attain. It's also like a "gaol," the British word for jail. Goals and resolutions always involve judgment. Have you made New Year's resolutions that didn't work out? And why didn't they work? Because they were based on judgments that you should be doing *this*—and this was the right and correct thing to do. You made a resolution, and you locked yourself into the jail of your judgment.

Resolutions are not based on an awareness of what actually is. And they're fixed in place; they're a fixed point of view. What happens when circumstances change? Will you have the awareness to realize that and take appropriate action—or will your attention remain fixed on your resolution?

Another difficulty with resolutions and goals is that they tend to lead to even more self-judgment. When we lock ourselves into a resolution or a goal, we're stuck with it even when circumstances change. For example, if you resolve to quit smoking by the end of the month, and you have a family member die or a crisis at work and smoking is one of the ways you manage stress, it might be unrealistic to expect yourself to quit during that time. And yet, if you have the resolution or goal to quit and you continue to smoke, you'll end up judging yourself harshly.

A more expansive approach is to let go of your goals and resolutions and choose targets for yourself instead. A target is something you can aim at; it can move and shift as you become aware of new possibilities.

Discernment. Judgment also shows up as discernment. In fact, *discernment* is defined as the ability to judge well. It's the process of selecting what's good, bad or worthwhile.

Discernment is also used in connection with discerning the will of God, which is about judging what is right or wrong. It is generally used as an excuse to not be aware of what's actually going on and to do whatever the heck you want to do. That's okay, as long as you're clear that you're choosing judgment over awareness.

A woman once came to see me who had just gotten into traditional recovery from a long-term cocaine addiction. She had been addicted to cocaine throughout her teenage daughter's life, and when the daughter was ten years old, she found her mother unconscious, overdosed and had to call to 911. There were other similar upsetting events throughout the daughter's life. I asked the woman, "What would it be like if we got some therapy for your daughter?"

The woman became outraged. She was clearly not willing to look at what her addiction might have created for her daughter. When she came back for her next session, she said, "I'm not going to work with you because I know that it's not God's will to have my daughter in therapy. She doesn't need it. I am just going to do this recovery program, and I don't need to ask any questions about what my addiction has been like for my daughter."

When someone uses discernment in that way, there's no point in arguing with him or her. They have already chosen and solidified what they decided is right and true. In this instance, I just wished the woman well and said goodbye.

Definition. When you define who you are and who you are not, you prevent yourself from changing and being anything and everything you can be—because you have gone into judgment.

I used to define myself as someone who couldn't handle big piles of paperwork. I needed somebody else to deal with them for me. I would say, "Paperwork is not my thing." When I looked back, I saw that I was told early on that I wasn't good at paperwork, and since it was not something I was interested in, I never developed the skill set for dealing with it. Recently I asked, "What would it take for me to develop the ability to handle piles of paperwork? Not that I might not still hire somebody to help me—but is that a possibility for me?" It was light.

So I started learning how to handle paperwork, and now I can actually deal with tall stacks of it. If I had remained in the judgment and definition of who I was—that I was not a person who could handle large amounts of paperwork—I never would have been able to change.

Defining yourself as anything, including an addict, is another way of limiting or diminishing yourself—because you are so much more than any definition you place on yourself. When you use awareness rather than definitions, you can do and be far more than you judge you can do and be. Please don't use definition to limit you.

Comparison. Comparison can also be a form of judgment. This is particularly true when comparison takes something that is complex and multi-dimensional, reduces it to one or two characteristics, and evaluates it against something else, which has been reduced in a similar fashion, and then arrives at a judgment about a whole, multi-faceted person or thing. These kinds of comparisons are misleading and meaningless because the context of the whole has been dropped out. They're a lie—or a misrepresentation—at best.

Comparing yourself to another person inevitably takes away and hides your absolute uniqueness. Is there anybody in the world that you could truly compare yourself to? There is not another you in the whole world—never has been, never will be. You are that special and unique. Any time you compare yourself to someone else, you have to judge yourself, contract yourself down and put yourself in the other person's universe, which inevitably diminishes you.

The other thing about comparisons is that they always depend on some external standard. I recently spoke with a young man who was attending a very competitive high school. Students' test scores were made public and the students compared their test results as though there was something meaningful about them. After the young man and I talked for a while, he began to see that the tests were an incomplete and inaccurate assessment of the people in his class. The tests did not even accurately predict students' academic potential. Even so, it was as if everyone had agreed the tests had some inherent validity or merit and that a student's ranking on the test in comparison to other students actually had some meaning.

Competition. Competition is a form of judgment that is heavily promoted in our culture. Most competition involves an attempt to beat or "best" someone else by achieving an arbitrary standard.

Even if you "win" the competition and "beat someone out," does that actually satisfy you? When you're doing competition, whether you've won the race, made the most money or showed up with the prettiest hairstyle, you have to continue to defend your title to make sure no one takes your win from you. Consider that as a way to live. You've completely limited the choices you have because of the energy it takes to constantly be on the lookout for anyone who might one-up you. And how much can you relax and show up as you when you're competing? If someone is competing with you, it can be very tempting to join the race. Without noticing, you can get tricked into competing with them. But you don't have to buy into it—if you're aware.

There is, however, one kind of competition that is generative, and that is competing with yourself. Competing with yourself is not about, "I have to be better," or "I have to get it right." It's more like, "I did it. That was fun. What else could I do?" You out-create yourself. It's expansive; judgment is not part of it. "I baked some interesting cookies. What other kind of cookies could I bake? What could I add to that recipe?" "I explored this section of town, even though I was a little scared to do it. Where else could I explore?" "Wow, I'm choosing to show up as me and I'm engaging less in my addictive or compulsive behavior. What could I do to increase that?"

The more you choose to be who you are, the less you buy into other people's realities—and that's what judgment does. It requires you to buy into somebody else's reality and judge yourself by their standards. What would it be like if you gave up all competition except the fun of out-creating yourself?

Significance. Making something significant always requires judgment. What do I mean by that? Here's an example: One day a huge red-tail hawk landed on the railing of my patio. I was thrilled to see it there, and I took some wonderful photos of it. When I showed them to people, some of them said things like, "Wow, a hawk is a totem—that has a lot of meaning."

It was tempting to make something "significant" out of the hawk's visit and to start thinking about what it meant, along the lines of, "This means I need to develop my hawk energy," or "What does the hawk's presence on my patio signify to me?" Fortunately, I didn't go there. Instead I was simply grateful for the gift of having this magnificent bird just ten feet away from me for a long period of time.

If you choose not to make things significant, you will have much more awareness and enjoyment in your life. True living is about the joy of being alive, being you and being aware. Any time you find yourself making something significant, ask, "If I didn't make this significant, what would I be aware of here?"

Shoulds, Ought To's and Obligations. All of the shoulds, ought to's and obligations in your life are arbitrary. They come from other people's points of view and judgments. "You should visit your mother more often." "You should not be so sexual." "You ought to help me whenever I ask you to." When you buy the shoulds, ought to's and obligations, you buy into the energy of contraction. You move into somebody else's reality and you give up having choice in your life.

"I'm obligated to be a good person." Really? According to whose definition of "good"? And what is a good person? Someone who is willing to lie down and be a doormat? "I am obligated to take care of certain family members." If that's light and expansive for you, if it honors you, then by all means, do it. But when it's light, it's not obligation. It's about your choice.

Obligations put you on automatic pilot. They remove choice and require you to act according to someone else's program. "I have obligations and they make up my entire life. I don't really exist, but that's okay because I am fulfilling my responsibilities, and obviously, I'm doing it right." It's all judgment.

When you become aware that you have stuck yourself with a should, an ought to or an obligation, ask:

- Okay, what is this?
- Whose idea is this?
- Who thinks I should be doing this or that I'm obligated to do it?
- Does it work for me?
- Does it give me more of me?
- Is it adding to my life?

If you've devoted yourself to taking care of all your family members so they don't have to take care of themselves, and you all of a sudden pull away from them and start making choices that truly work for you, you may be judged as selfish. It's often the judgments of others that keep us coming back to shoulds, ought to's and obligations. Be aware of that, and don't buy the idea that because you are taking care of yourself, you are self-centered or egotistical. It's actually the opposite. When you are being you, you are on the track to becoming the gift you are to the world.

And when you are being you, you'll be less drawn to engage in addictive or compulsive behavior. Instead, you'll choose to take good care of yourself and your body, and to make the choices that expand your life, even during stressful times.

Epilogue

L eaving addiction behind is a journey that takes enormous courage. If you are choosing this, please be kind to you. As you begin to let go of limiting belief systems and the "shoulds," "oughts"
and responsibilities you've been programed with, you may encounter resistance from others, or even from yourself. You will be going
against the norm and often what's considered good and right. Please
remember that you and only you can know what's actually going
to expand your life. Learning that you can trust yourself to know
what you know, to know what the correct action for you to take
in any given situation, can take awhile. There may be many starts
and stops, as well as discouragement and anxiety. I encourage you
to keep going. The greatest gift you can give yourself and the world
is to show up as who you really are, with all of the parts and pieces
you have deemed unacceptable back in place. When you do this,
addiction cannot exist. Addiction can only be present when you are
not being you.

Many clients have expressed their concern to me: What if I'm
a terrible person? What if the only way to keep me from doing bad
things is to operate from judgment? You're not and it isn't. When
you begin to live your life from what you know to be true for you,

rather than from all of the various forms of judgment that have been heaped upon you, there is an incredible energy of lightness and expansiveness that is a contribution to all. What if you could be the inspiration to others rather than just another cog on the wheel? You showing up as you not only frees you from addiction, it allows others to see that there is a different way. Being the greatness of you can be a bit daunting. It probably goes against everything you've decided is true about you, but how much fun could that be? How much more joy and expansion and choice and possibility are you willing to have? The invitation is there. What will you choose?

Definition of Addiction:

Addiction is an entrenched pattern of avoidance and/or escape from a life that appears to be too overwhelming and painful. It is a place people go to not exist and to not experience the pain of self judgment and the sense of being inherently wrong. It is a flight from the imagined or false self, into a contracted place of existence. Whether it's alcohol or food or being a victim or over working, the individual finds something to escape with or into, then erroneously decides that the substance or activity is necessary and required in order to survive. Choice is sacrificed for the lie of dependence, and the individual begins a self-perpetuating cycle where he/she becomes increasingly diminished. From this place it is easy to believe that there is no possibility of release or recovery.

However, because the assumptions underlying the path to addiction are based on misinformation, inaccurate conclusions and decisions, real recovery is possible. Addiction is not a life sentence or an identity. It is a created behavioral pattern, and with accurate information and tools, anyone can come to a place of real choice with any behavior. As individuals are empowered to claim more and more of who they are, the addictive behavior loses its pull and the individual is free to create a life they truly desire.

Resources

To contact Marilyn or find out more about the Right Recovery
for You program visit:
www.rightrecoveryforyou.com

To find out more about Access Consciousness® or to locate
an Access Consciousness® facilitator in your area, visit:
www.accessconsciousness.com

For more information about the Access Consciousness®
clearing statement, visit:
www.theclearingstatement.com

About the Author

Marilyn Bradford, MSSW, MEd., CFMW, is an international speaker, psychotherapist and teacher who has worked in the field of addiction for over twenty years. She is the director of Right Recovery For You, a radical and unique approach to ending any addictive or compulsive behavior. It was her own addictions to alcohol, food and the wrongness of self, and her unwillingness to accept addiction as a life sentence, that led her to creating this transformative and very different program.

Growing up in an academic family that stressed the supreme value of logic and the scientific method, Marilyn knew from an early age that she was not going to fit well in this world. She was a square peg in a round hole. What others took for granted seemed insane to her. This was the beginning of the sense of fundamental wrongness of self that eventually led to escape through food, alcohol and adapting to other people's realities.

At the time, there didn't seem to be any other alternatives. Some instances of abuse added to the desire to escape. After years of addiction, Marilyn entered a traditional treatment program. While it was helpful in quitting alcohol, the emphasis on powerless, wrongness and the label of alcoholic became unacceptable to her. She knew somehow that she and others she met in the program had creative and generative capacities that were being denied and damaged by the prevailing belief systems concerning addiction.

While searching for alternatives, she was introduced to Access Consciousness®. Here she found pragmatic tools and techniques that she could use to empower herself and others to move beyond the limiting belief systems that prevail. Seeing the vast improvement in her psychotherapy/addiction clients that came from using these tools, she approached Gary Douglas, the founder of Access Consciousness®, and together they founded Right Recovery For You.

Now she travels the world offering others a chance for true freedom from addiction.

Right Recovery for You Workshops
A Radical New Approach for
Ending Addiction Fast

Right Recovery for You (RRFY) is a radically different approach for freeing people from addiction, faster and with less energy than any other traditional program. It is NOT therapy. It is NOT addiction management. It is about ENDING addiction completely, once and for all.

While Alcoholics Anonymous requires lifelong attendance, Right Recovery For You can move people to a place of choice with their addictive behaviour and heal people's pain around addictions (drugs, food, sex, gambling, work, illness, victim mentality) in as little as six sessions.

Co-founder of RRFY, Marilyn Bradford, MSSW, CFMW, MEd., is an international speaker and teacher who has worked in the field of addiction recovery for more than twenty years. She has also successfully overcome her own addictions to alcohol and cigarettes.

"Right Recovery tools and techniques have been able to end the pain and confusion of addiction with more ease, less time and energy, and without a pathological label that sticks to one for life,"

Marilyn says. "It treats the core of the problem, not just the symptoms, for complete recovery."

What's so different about the Right Recovery for You approach?

1. Addiction is not a disease

Unlike other programs, RRFY states that addiction is NOT a disease, it's just a series of personal choices based on lack of information and appropriate life skills and tools. An addict chooses destructive talk, negative-feelings and conclusion about themselves and life.

2. Creating choice not abstinence

RRFY does NOT require people to give up their chosen substance or process. Instead, it successfully empowers individuals to come to a place of complete choice so they have the freedom, for example, to drink or not to drink.

3. NO label of addict

RRFY never labels people as addicts. Instead, RRFY sees the addiction as a behaviour that will come to an end when an individual has the right knowledge and life tools to make a new and more empowering behavioural choice.

4. Discovery of the primary vs secondary addictions

Marilyn's discovery that there is a primary addiction to judgment and the wrongness of self, has assisted her clients in even faster transformation. The primary addiction is always hovering below any secondary addiction such as alcohol, sex or gambling. Without clearing this primary addiction, relapse and struggle with other addictions are common.

5. An empowering set of questions and tools

Most people with addictive behaviours look at what is wrong with themselves. RRFY uses strategic questions and tools to empower clients to work with and end their addictions, including the following:

What's right about your addiction you're not getting? Addictions always provide a benefit to the person stuck in the behaviour —e.g. a smoker gets a break from work.

- Who does this belong to? Most of our thoughts, feelings and emotions don't actually belong to

- Who does this belong to? Most of our thoughts, feelings and emotons don't actually belong to us. A great question to ask is: Who are you drinking for? Or spending for? Or eating for? Or being abused for?*

- Is this heavy or light? If it's light, it's right. If it's heavy, it's a lie. Using the heavy and light tool teaches people to trust themselves again, and stop buying other people's version of life for them.*

- Do something different every day. All addictive and compulsive behaviors are habits of magnitude. Developing the muscle of making different choices empowers people to have more choice around their behavior.

- Let of guilt, shame, regret. Guilt, shame and regret are unnatural learned states that feed addiction. What if you were willing to let go of them?

NOTE: Questions marked with an asterisk are tools that come directly from Access Consciousness®

For more information and to contact Marilyn Bradford visit:

Scan for more information

Testimonials

Marilyn Bradford saved my life. I was spending about $500 to $1000 a week on cocaine and not sleeping for a week at a time. It was the darkest time in my life. That is when I was referred to Marilyn. After seeing Marilyn for six weeks, I broke my daily habit for the first time in several years. Marilyn gave me the tools to cure my addiction and create the life I have always wanted. Today, I am living happy and free from cocaine addiction.

CC, Texas

Marilyn Bradford opens all the doors. I spent years in Twelve Step programs for numerous addictions. Admitting I was powerless felt like admitting I was wrong. Marilyn has helped me recognize that I was addicted to being wrong, that being wrong was actually a comfortable place for me. It was a place that kept me stuck in old habits. Marilyn's facilitation and processes have given me the insights and freedom to clear these habits and addictions. Now anything is possible. All the doors are open.

M. L., Australia

Marilyn is a gentle and intelligent facilitator. She has a gift of knowing and distilling (from her vast repertoire) the exact kernel you require, to empower you to make the changes you're ready for at that moment. It's clear that the techniques she teaches come from personal experience. Marilyn knows what works.

M-J, Korea/Australia

Marilyn is able to brilliantly add the Access tools and technologies to her knowledge and wisdom regarding addictions for an incredible impact! This not only shifts things in the physical reality regarding addictive behavior, but changes the energetic patterns holding belief systems and past programming in place (which includes family patterns taken on at an early age) that makes addictions so difficult to eliminate using only traditional methods normally used in our society. If you really would choose to totally eliminate any kind of addictive behavior, this is your ticket to a new YOU!

D. O., Tennessee

I have been a part of one of Marilyn's tele-classes, and I have also taken part in one-on-one sessions with her. What I love about Marilyn is her authenticity, and her willingness to use the Access tools, while at the same time hold me to using the tools too. She walks her talk. Expect results with her, she doesn't waste yours or her time.

L. L., Minnesota

Marilyn has an amazing knowledge of addiction of all kinds of behaviors, how it keeps you stuck and how you can start changing it. I am always flabbergasted by all the information and aha moments I receive on her calls on the Puja network and the tele-series Ending the Primary Addiction—Judgment and the Wrongness of Self. She presents her in-

depth knowledge in a very clear way, with humor, and I find her a very empowering facilitator.

C. M., Netherlands

I am so grateful for Marilyn and the contribution she has been to changing so much in my world. I have been participating recently in the 'Ending The Primary Addiction' tele-call. Throughout these calls she has been the invitation for me stepping into more of me. Don't ask me to explain how.........it's just like magic really! Her willingness to follow the energy and to be in total allowance of each person participating has been such a gift. I know this has provided a space for me to feel comfortable asking questions and being more vulnerable. Thank you, Marilyn, for all that you be. I am brimming with gratitude!

F. S., New Zealand

Marilyn is brilliant. Her willingness to explore the world of addiction outside the box takes us past the hopelessness and destruction into possibilities for living. Marilyn's experience and her constant quest for information combine with her intuitive knowing, her caring and her kindness to empower each of us to step up, take charge and live our own life.

D. N., Minnesota

From the first time I met Marilyn—I knew that she had a "special" something. When I was going through therapy years ago, I wished I had someone like Marilyn to go to. She's kind, caring and brilliant in her facilitation. And, don't be fooled—she is laser sharp and can call you on your "stuff" and empowers you to "know that you know." She's like the kind, aware, empowering mom that I wish I had growing up. In the classes and tele-classes I've taken with her, I've felt that she had my "back" and that I could be vulnerable and tell her anything because she is in allowance and doesn't judge. How did I get so lucky?

With gratitude,

L. W., Colorado

Although I am not a native English speaker, I always felt I was really heard in the tele-class with Marilyn. I didn't feel judged by her, and therefore I opened myself to the greater changes that have occurred and she was there with me. And I also knew she was there for each person on the call. Amazing! I first came up contracted, with a sense of heaviness all around me. She gave me the Access tools which I did use. Today I feel light. I have a sense of more space and peace. I sleep better. My head is not spinning around anymore. And I feel good about myself. Thank you, Marilyn!

N. C., Rio de Janeiro, Brazil

Other Access Consciousness® Books

Being You, Changing the World

By Dr. Dain Heer

Have you always known that something COMPLETELY DIF-FERENT is possible? What if you had a handbook for infinite possibilities and dynamic change to guide you? With tools and processes that actually worked and invited you to a completely different way of being? For you? And the world?

The Ten Keys to Total Freedom

By Gary M. Douglas & Dr. Dain Heer

The Ten Keys to Total Freedom are a way of living that will help you expand your capacity for consciousness so that you can have greater awareness about yourself, your life, this reality and beyond. With greater awareness you can begin creating the life you've always known was possible but haven't yet achieved. If you will actually do and be these things, you will get free in every aspect of your life.

Embodiment:
The Manual You Should Have Been Given
When You Were Born

By Dr. Dain Heer

The information you should have been given at birth, about bodies, about being you and what is truly possible if you choose it…What if your body were an ongoing source of joy and greatness? This book introduces you to the awareness that really is a different choice for you—and your sweet body.

Right Body for You

By Gary M. Douglas and Donnielle Carter

This is a very different perspective about bodies and your ability to change yours. It might all be easier than you ever knew was possible! *Right Body for You* is a book that will inspire you and show you a different way of creating the body you truly desire.

Pragmatic Psychology:
Practical Tools For Being Crazy Happy

By Susanna Mittermaier

Everyone has at least one "crazy" person in their life, right (even if it's ourselves!)? And there are a lot of labels and diagnoses out there—depression, anxiety, ADD, ADHD, bi-polar, schizophrenia…What if there was a different possibility with mental illness—and what if change and happiness were a totally available reality? Susanna is a clinical psychologist with an amazing capacity to facilitate what this reality often defines as crazy from a totally different point of view—one of possibility and ease.

Divorceless Relationships
By Gary M. Douglas

Most of us spend a lot of time divorcing parts and pieces of ourselves in order to care for someone else. For example, you like to go jogging but instead of jogging, you spend that time with your partner to show him or her that you really care. "I love you so much that I would give up this thing that is valuable to me so I can be with you." This is one of the ways you divorce you to create an intimate relationship. How often does divorcing you really work in the long run?

Beyond the Stigma of Abuse
By Linda Wasil

If you've tried everything and are still "stuck" or searching, please join me for a totally different way of dealing with the issues of abuse. This book will not be like anything you have previously read, heard or bought as true about abuse. What if this is the information you've been asking for?

Leading from the Edge of Possibility:
No More Business as Usual
By Chutisa and Steven Bowman

Just imagine what your business and your life would be like if you stopped functioning on autopilot and began to generate your business with strategic awareness and prosperity consciousness. This is truly possible, except you have to be willing to change. Recognizing a different possibility requires a different mindset and almost always demands a kind of awareness that is not part of prior experience. With this book you'll get the awareness you need to lead your business in any environment!

Joy of Business

By Simone Milasas

If you were creating your business from the JOY of it—what would you choose? What would you change? What would you choose if you knew you could not fail? Business is JOY, it's creation, it's generative. It can be the adventure of LIVING.

CPSIA information can be obtained at www.ICGtesting.com
Printed in the USA
LVOW08s0659250115

424183LV00002B/6/P